MANIFESTOS FOR THE 21ST CENTURY

SERIES EDITORS: URSULA OWEN AND JUDITH VIDAL-HALL

This series began with free expression as its central theme, arising at a time when the problems of censorship and offence were very much centre stage. As it has developed over the years the Manifesto series has expanded to include questions of rights, liberties, tolerance, silencing, dissent and other major issues of our day. The distinguished authors, some of the world's sharpest analysts and foremost thinkers, address a wide range of themes, from trust to equality, from multiculturalism to the Israel–Palestine conflict, from the condition of Europe to the nature of offence.

We live in a world where people with widely different cultural habits and beliefs live in proximity, where words, images and behaviour come under the closest scrutiny and are fiercely debated. In such a complex and precarious world, these books aim to surprise, clarify and provoke in equal measure.

MANIFESTOS FOR THE 21ST CENTURY

END OF EQUALITY
The Only Way Is Women's Liberation

BEATRIX CAMPBELL

LONDON NEW YORK CALCUTTA

Seagull Books, 2013

© Beatrix Campbell, 2013

ISBN   978 0 85742 1 135

British Library Cataloguing-in-Publication Data
A catalogue record for this book is available
from the British Library

Typeset and designed by Seagull Books, Calcutta, India
Printed and bound by Hyam Enterprises, Calcutta, India

For Callum, Jude, Joe, Amelie and Beth
with love

CONTENTS

Acknowledgements

The text was read and sometimes reread, and improved by Doreen Massey, Liz Kelly, Rahila Gupta, Stuart Hall, Miranda Horvath, Elizabeth Mansfield, Sharon Mier and by Judith Jones who enhances everything.

This work has benefited from conversations and interviews with Eliane Vogel-Polsky, John Bercow, Yvette Cooper, Janet Veitch, Sue Himmelweit, Jonathan Gershuny, Oriel Sullivan, Diane Elson, Louise Carlin, Rosina McRae, Carol Fox, Peter Murphy, Peter Doyle, Stefan Cross, Christine Wharrier, Stuart Hill, Sue Hastings, Karon Monaghan, Robin Allen, Daphne Romney, Betsy Stanko, Adah Kay, Fiona McTaggart, Sally Morgan, Joan Ruddock, Hazel Blears, Jo Morris, Daniel Finkelstein, Trish Morris, Delia Davin, Gail Hershatter, Sophie Gamwell, Charlie Whelan,

Ceri Goddard, Angela Eagle, Andrea Murray, Sylvie Tissot and Sophie Pirkin.

I'm immensely grateful for the support of the Amiel Melburn and Scurragh Wainwright trusts.

A NEW SEXUAL SETTLEMENT

Women's liberation is dead. Long live women's liberation. Women's liberation changed lives. To paraphrase Karl Marx's words in the introduction to the best-known manifesto in the world, the *Manifesto of the Communist Party*:[1]

> A spectre is haunting the world: the spectre is a woman, any woman, women. All the powers of old Europe and the old world have entered into a holy alliance to exorcize this spectre. Their branding reproach is that women are already equal to men, and if not yet equal, then all but [. . .] Or that equality has already gone too far, that men are unmanned, that it is an offence

against nature. By their complacency
or their contempt, the holy alliance
hails the spectre as if it were already
a power in the new world.

Marx wrote about a working class whose
revolutionary potential is conjured in the
nightmare of its enemies. Feminism is simi-
larly accused—as if it were a power in the
world. And of course it is—as ideas, as
desires, as a cultural revolution, as movements, as relationships, as laws and mani-
festos—and it is not. Within a decade or so
of the birth of women's liberation at the end
of the 1960s, the conditions enabling it were
ebbing away. Its beginning was also the
beginning of the end.

Nowhere does the 'spectre' run governments. Nowhere have men en masse been
persuaded to share power, time, money,
resources and respect equally with women.
Women did not create this state of affairs, nor
did they consent to it. Yet, in the twenty-first
century the prevailing faith is that the age of
patriarchy is over, the world's institutions have

given up on it; women are winning and feminism, therefore, is passé;[2] and if women aren't there yet then it is only a matter of evolution. But evolution towards equality is a fiction and a fraud. Women are not evolutionary failures. Men seized the means of organization, men made the world's political systems and parties in their own interests and men still speak to women with forked tongue.

Sojourner Truth, who was born into slavery and became one of the great activists against slavery and for the vote, had cautioned the American Equal Rights Association in 1867: 'Man is so selfish that he has got women's rights and his own too [. . .]. He keeps them all to himself.'[3]

A century later, black and white women involved in freedom rides, sit-ins and marches for black civil rights and against the US war in Vietnam, had to overcome the selfishness again and find their voice: their ardent manifesto, insisting that 'this is no more a man's world than it is a white world,'[4] became a founding text of the women's liberation movement. Women created a new political terrain which was seeded by their resistance to racism, war and sexism.

But women's liberation had scarcely danced onto the stage before the world was captured by capitalism's second coming. A new historical settlement is shaping the world: neopatriarchal neoliberalism, an ugly name for an ugly deal. It has been a hostile climate for feminism: it didn't thrive,[5] but it didn't die; it survives, it is nowhere and everywhere—and the phoenix is flying again.

Old Times, New Times

Gender doesn't explain everything but it is *in* all of human life: gender is omni-relevant, it is decisive in organizing social difference and in conditioning the exercise of power.[6] All of us, every man, woman and child, are 'doing gender':[7] in every flicker of an eyelid and every penny we spend, save or owe; in every teardrop and every bottom wiped or pinched; in every pail of water hauled, microchip fabricated and oil well blown; and in every political decision that favours private gain over public good.

Twenty-first century capitalism presents itself as liberation logic: it pitches choice and competition against the dependency, mutuality and co-operation that are the conditions of life itself. It shrinks the space of politics and, thus, the possibility of challenge and change. It recoils from social solidarity and shared care and, thus, from rapport with women. Whatever its specific political form, whether Anglo-American or post-dictatorship South American neoliberalism or Chinese state-sponsored capitalism, it is neopatriarchal theory and practice—it does not liberate women.

Global fiscal policies do not audit the unpaid work that makes the world go round: the un-priced and priceless work of care, estimated at between one-third and half of GDP. Feminist scholars Sue Himmelweit and Hilary Land spell it out: to treat care as just a cost, to withdraw support from care is the 'transfer of resources (unpaid labour) from women to relieve taxpayers, disproportionately men'.[8]

Global financial policies are freezing gender pay gaps and time gaps. Economic equality is impossible in labour markets differentiated by men's time and mothers' time, with women bearing overwhelming responsibility for the labours of love. Men have now been doing more domestic work and care than they did but not much more—at best at a rate of *one minute more per day per year*.

Women are now better educated and better qualified than men in *all* categories of work, but unequal pay and power begins at the beginning and gets worse over a lifetime.[9] Inspired arithmetic calculates that a snail would have slithered round London's M25 motorway nine times in the 50 years it would take to achieve equality in the judiciary.[10] A snail might just about traverse the Great Wall of China in the 212 years it would take to attain gender parity in Westminster's Parliament. But a snail's lifespan, the hazards of the M25 motorway and 5,500 miles of the wall suggests another scenario—that we'll all be dead.

Neoliberalism not only generates inequality but also radiates violence. Where its writ runs, societies are troubled and violent. Millions live in the precarious mayhem of slums patrolled by militias, sheriffs and gangs, where crime and armed conflict, insurgency and counterinsurgency make, and are maintained by, violent masculinity.

Millions of women live in societies where violence or death is the penalty for answering back, loving another man, loving a woman, giving birth, going to school. Two women die every week in England because some man whom some woman doesn't love anymore simply wants to kill her. More than hundred million women are missing worldwide, dead from neglect.[11]

This new articulation[12] of capitalism and patriarchy is hegemonic. That does not make it stable: all over the world there is tumult and resistance. Feminist politics is always contingent and constrained, always ebbing and flowing, permanently rustling the culture even if intermittently expressed as *politics* because, of course, it comes out of subordination, it is mediated, re-interpreted and it is formidably opposed.

History has not been on the side of women—but feminism is an optimistic politics.

MONEY

The Bonus

In 2008, for the first time in decades, the words capitalism, crisis and class could be spoken in sequence in polite society without seeming passé. Citizens' wrath was steered to the banking industry's most conspicuous signifier: the bonus.

The bonus represented startling continuity in regimes of remuneration between the old smoky capitalism and the purportedly hygienic capitalism of the twenty-first century, when finance finally ruled the world. Bonuses are not wages. They are bribes—but bribes that pose as rewards. They belong to a repertoire of remuneration that, like the industry itself, is indecently obscure—the antithesis of democracy. Their purpose is to broadcast hierarchies and the *necessity* of inequality, and to disguise the collaborative context of work.[13]

Bankers cannot get through a working day without toilets, food, administration, computers and colleagues. They cannot get to work without transport; they cannot leave their children without carers; they cannot compute without hardware and software from California and China; and they cannot do their work without the collective intelligence of others. They cannot become bankers without education. They would die without nurses and doctors, and they would die without love.

Even before the crisis, women who cleaned toilets and women who traded information about stocks and shares, women who were paid from £10,000 to £300,000 a year, were trying to expose the bonus as a vector of excess, secrecy and sexism.

When the UK's New Labour government gave the City its benediction it defined the national interest by only 'one square mile of it'[14] and championed 'one of the last bastions of male privilege'—where women spent their working lives weaving and dodging sexist culture outlawed elsewhere—'virtually untouched by the legal and social changes which have been occurring outside it'. The City was a place where women 'put up and shut up'.[15]

Some did not shut up. City analyst Louise Barton, who earned £100,000 a year and £300,000 as bonus, launched a pioneering legal attack in 2003 after learning that her junior male colleague received £1,000,000 as bonus. Her case ought to have detonated the industry's sexism and secrecy. It did not.[16]

Executive directors in the 1990s earned twice their basic salary through bonuses. By the crash in 2008, they were earning four times their salary through bonuses. By 2013, bonuses had stalled but salaries made up less than one-third of their incomes, and the City—comprising fewer than 5 per cent of Britain's workers—took over one-third of all bonuses.[17] The bonus gender gap among managers is a spectacular 80 per cent.[18]

The City is addicted to mystical performance criteria[19] immune from scrutiny because companies do not bother to collect statistics.[20] Ignorance, idiosyncrasy, bias and stereotypes saturate employers' discretion. Inequality is inevitable and intended.

An Unsuitable Case

Public service is not a suitable case for the bonus. The public sector is women's best hope of equal pay.[21] But in an early transfusion of market values, bonuses were introduced in 1971 to raise *men's* pay and productivity—at the same time when employers and unions were supposed to implement the 1970 Equal Pay Act.[22] Did no one think twice?

A kind of collective larceny was perpetrated against millions of women. It took another quarter of a century before the public sector even began to implement equal pay.[23] After yet another decade—when the global economic crisis put public service itself in jeopardy—two-thirds of local authorities had still not delivered.[24] This caused an epic crisis of comeuppance. Disgusted by both employers' and unions' bad faith, some women sued local authorities, and unions too, for manipulating and misleading them.

Finally, the labour movement moved.[25] In 2006, women working in the health service in the border county of Cumbria won the UK's biggest ever settlement—£300,000,000. They had to withstand union pressure to settle swiftly for much less—until lawyers warned that the union itself might be sued. When the women won the biggest pay deal ever they expected national officials to join their celebration. No one did.

By now, at least employers and unions knew what they had to do—the right thing. But the right thing was not done: many of the Cumbrian women did not get the full amount. No one would explain why. It was as if their legal entitlement was an embarrassing excess. And the right thing did not stop some public bodies spending fortunes doing the wrong thing: on defending unequal pay and patriarchal perks that were, of course, still flaunted in the City.

A de facto cartel of 20 councils in Scotland resisted nursery nurses and teaching assistants all the way to the Supreme Court in 2013—and lost. Birmingham, Europe's biggest local authority, defended a deal at the expense of 5,000 women that gave men doing equivalent work bonuses that were bigger than a woman's annual salary. The women won but not before a six-week tribunal where 20 solicitors and half a dozen barristers (on US$450 an hour) navigated through 200 files of evidence going back 30 years and 15,000 documents that mysteriously appeared just before the hearing.

The case resurfaced when women who had been excluded because they'd left the council before the case was taken, appealed and won.[26] Again, no one with any power raised a glass to these women: yet another strange silence.[27]

The bonus rewarded men for being there, for handling machines rather than people, for doing what they were paid to do, for any old thing—simply for being men. These huge deals threw startling light on what women had lost.

The UK government had allowed local councils to set aside US$300 million to settle; they actually needed US$6 billion. In Birmingham alone equal-pay cases cost the council an estimated £890 million—with more to come—and the council was forced to contemplate selling off assets after the government refused to help bail it out.[28] Governments bailed out reckless banks but refused to bail out councils for institutional sexism.

The political system did not learn from the women, it blamed them. Their success was deemed 'a bad day for unions'. Chris Mullin, Labour MP for Sunderland South, told Parliament in 2007 that deals should be forced on women. Their lawyers, he spat, were parasites.[29] Some Labour men sound like Tories, weighing women's legal *rights* against men's *privileges* and relying on past sexism to extenuate future sexism.

Conversations with cabinet ministers confirmed their priorities, 'Such an enormous cost,' confided one minister, 'we just can't afford it.' 'Equal pay? We didn't think about it,' recalled a Downing Street insider.

Mullin's spite was aimed at carers, caterers and cleaners—women whose stories, aired within the bland walls of tribunals, disclose how the economic is never only economic, how so many women's encounters with equality have been furtive, rough and disappointing, how millions of women have lived on so little, how rarely their pride in taking care of people, 'the public', their hospitals, cities and councils has been reciprocated. Here was a horrible clarity about what mattered. Men mattered.

Crumbling Paradigm

All this should make women 'deeply, deeply angry,' says Robin Allen, QC, doyen of gruelling equalities activism in the courts.

The biggest breach in Britain's gender pay gap happened in the middle of the 1970s when implementation of the 1970 Equal Pay Act converged with a uniquely egalitarian national pay agreement, the Social Contract, between trade unions and the Labour government. But it was a historic one-off, the last time any UK government endorsed equality.

Equal pay is a concept in need of clarification. It was first inscribed in European law as a sexist manoeuvre *against* women. In the 1960s, a young Belgian human rights lawyer, Eliane Vogel-Polsky, disinterred this ugly history. Exasperated by political inertia, she excavated the equality protocols that developed from the 1919 Treaty of Versailles and the International Labour Organization (ILO) to which it gave birth, and which were later adopted by the European Common Market and the United Nations (UN).

The ILO had ensured that equal pay be inscribed in international law at the behest of trade union men. Vogel-Polsky later met some of them: 'Men believed that if employers were obliged to pay women the same as men, of course, they would take the men. It was the old patriarchal model,' she told me in an interview. 'The men wanted it in to defend their own rights. So, it was not a feminist idea!'[30] This 'patriarchal model' found its way into Article 119 of the 1957 Treaty of Rome.

But Vogel-Polsky had invoked it *for women* and she was vindicated in 1976 when the European Court of Justice ruled that Article 119 should apply to all states and agreements. She became a heroine in European equality politics. The experience taught her that nothing less than 'total legal and activist commitment was needed'.

Trade unions were both indispensable and 'awful'—they had taken the side of men; the law was indispensable but it had been written by and for men. 'The equal pay law was programmed to be *not* achieved.' It did not address women's lives or gender generally. 'Now,' she despairs, 'neoliberalism is doing its work everywhere, and for women that is a defeat.'

17

Women are now better educated than men, but it doesn't matter—whatever they do they still get paid less than men. In the UK, full-timers' hourly pay gap decreased by about 1 per cent a year until flattening in the 2000s at around 20 per cent.[31] The part-time hourly pay gap remained bleakly static at around 40 per cent—this is women's parenting pay penalty—hourly rates disguise the real gap over a week, a year and a lifetime. In Europe, full-timers' annual gender pay gap is 26 per cent and between part-time women and full-time men—the defining difference—65 per cent. At retirement, men's pensions are 50 per cent higher than women's.[32]

The pay gap seems permanent. Employment scholars Damian Grimshaw and Jill Rubery warn that it is not a 'legacy effect': ongoing 'dynamics of undervaluation', new organizational forms, 'create new opportunities for undervaluation'.[33] The European Commission reports no 'significant increase for several years'.[34] US experts report that the 'rate of convergence slowed markedly in the

1990s'.[35] The ILO notes that a new gender gap is growing, based on inequality in the quality of employment.[36] 'Gender justice' is impossible in an 'inherently male' economy that does not integrate paid and unpaid domestic work or men's and women's differential bargaining power in public and private, says the ILO, women should not be forced to fit a masculine economy, we need a 'new gender approach,' a 'broader paradigm'.[37]

TIME

The pay gap is embedded in politics of time. Patriarchal modernity has made men, women and children live by different clocks and timetables. The 'working week' has been institutionalized in the interests of men unencumbered by duties of care. Politics, not biology, made the modern breadwinner a man, a provider rather than a parent and partner.[38]

'Private' and 'free' time is neither private nor free. Time is disciplined by the daily seasons of work and the needs of others. The power to *take* women's time is a resource for both patriarchy and capitalism. Although the old sexual settlement is *un*settled, unsustainable, it is reinstated: women's presence in the world of waged work is permanent yet always contingent on *taking care of care*.

A feminist politics of time was first brought to my mind by the women sewing machinists at Ford's car factory in Dagenham in the 1970s, when their unions formulated a novel annual claim that stretched beyond pay to time and the social wage. I was a young reporter interested in what this meant for women whose strike over skill and equal pay brought the mighty Ford to a standstill and made history in 1968. They talked about time: time off, control over their time, paid time that synchronized with their unpaid domestic time and with life. They were regarded as militant but they mystified union leaders to whom money, not time, was real politics.

The politics of time was clarified in my women's liberation group in the 1970s when one of us, a mother of small children, found herself single. Parenting *and* providing seemed irreconcilable.[39] Within a generation it had become the norm. By 2010 single parents comprised 25 per cent of all families and 60 per cent had a paid job. The agenda this implies is obvious: not the trick of work–life balance that assigns responsibility to women but a political economy that has at its heart not a breadwinner who is an unencumbered, cared-for man but a mother.

Women's appeal to men to share parenting has, of course, been answered by millions of men. They attend the birth of their babies, they fall in love with them and then soon, too soon, before they have even got acquainted, they leave the babies and the mothers from morning till night and go back to their paid jobs. Nowhere have men reciprocated women's paid work and unpaid care by initiating mass movements for *men's* equal parental leave or working time that synchronizes with children and women; nowhere have men en masse shared the costs—in time and money—of childhood.

In Britain—exemplar of Anglo-American neoliberalism—55 per cent of mothers are employed for short hours and 40 per cent of fathers for long hours, the most pronounced time gap in Europe.[40] Part-time pay is routinely regarded as not a real wage.[41]

How much men share care is a subject of wistful optimism and torrid conflict within households. How much change means real change?[42] From the 1970s to the 2000s, men's core daily domestic work—cleaning and cooking—increased by a rate of about *one minute per day per year* (see Table 1).[43] In the case of full-time employed heterosexual couples, two-thirds of women do much more

TABLE 1
UK Men and Women's Core Daily Domestic Labour in Minutes

YEAR	MEN	WOMEN
1975	20	197
2004	53	146

housework than men and one-third of men do a bit more than women. Typically, the sexual segregation of tasks 'is intensified over the life course'.[44]

We can infer that the pace of change is simultaneously palpable and pitiful.

Men and Children

From the 1970s to the 2000s, men's overall average time doing dedicated childcare (that is when they're not doing something else at the same time, surfing the net or watching football) increased by about 10 minutes a day—a rate of about *30 seconds per day per year* for three decades (see Table 2).[45]

TABLE 2

The Average Minutes Per Day Devoted by Men to Childcare in the UK, the US and Norway

DECADE	UK	US	NORWAY
1970s	10	11	13
2000s	17	23	22

Women's overall primary childcare increased more than men's, everywhere (see Table 3).

The Average Minutes Per Day Devoted by Women to Childcare in the UK, the US and Norway

DECADE	UK	US	NORWAY
1970s	26	48	47
2000s	42	52	55

In London's Square Mile, the politics of time is proudly patriarchal—it produces the misery of men with no other life. The former governor of the Bank of England, Mervyn King, told a Parliamentary committee, 'One of the things I found somewhat distressing about the lives of many people who worked in the City was that to many of them the purpose of a bonus and compensation was to give them a chance to leave the City.'[46] Of City workers with young children,

70 per cent work 10-hour days plus over-
time.[47]

South Korea and Japan exemplify how
the time gender gap causes demographic crisis. Men do little or no housework: in Japan
43 per cent of married men and in South
Korea 33 per cent do none at all. Women's
presence in the labour market is low and the
gender pay gap is high.[48] These modern
patriarchies have thin welfare systems (Korea
spends 7 per cent compared to the Organization for Economic Co-operation and Development [OECD] average of 20 per cent): long
working hours, low levels of public childcare,
and fertility rates below the level needed for
these societies to reproduce themselves.[49]

All categories of mothers in Europe and
North America in the twenty-first century
do more childcare than full-time mothers
did during the supposedly golden age of
modern patriarchy in the 1950s.[50] Contrary
to mournful laments that baby boomers are
selfish and slack absentees, that mothers
are to blame for the bad behaviour of boys,

for empty fridges and empty communities, women's long march into paid work is not a march away from children.

Everything Changes

The evidence challenges myths that divisions of labour are 'natural' or 'rational' and that change is slow but steady. In fact, there has been *unsteady* change in different directions. In China, three decades of capitalism created widening 'unfair' and 'unsustainable' differentials between men and women.[51] Finland had the world's highest ratio of full-time working women (part-time jobs are rare) and world-class public childcare.[52] The synergy of sexism and privatization eroded that. In the 1980s, right-wing pressure produced a modest cash allowance as a cheap alternative. When recession hit Finland, women under 35 were hit harder than anywhere else in Europe: 30 per cent became jobless and 26 per cent were put on short-term contracts.[53] Women—but not men—of family-forming age were targeted.[54] This drastically reduced the number of children in day care.[55] The global prognosis is bleak. Even the optimistic time-use expert Oriel Sullivan admits that progress is 'too significant, if slow' to belittle, but that a radical surge is 'hard to imagine'.

Neoliberalism Is Sexist

Any doubts that neoliberal economics is patriarchal were vanquished in the British Conservative–Liberal Democrat government's 2010 austerity budget. It allocated 72 per cent of the financial burden to women and 28 per cent to men. That was before planned cuts in public services. This violent redistribution away from women and children was the biggest in the history of the welfare state, said Labour MP Yvette Cooper: she had carried the budget around with her, calculator and computer to hand, auditing every detail.

Her analysis was framed by a new constitutional duty: the 2006 Equality Act required public authorities to proactively promote equality, to have 'due regard' in all policy-making to the impact on gender (and other grounds) and to mitigate any negative effects.[56] These duties had the potential to transcend the limits of the old equality paradigm by obliging all public policymaking to be disciplined by the duty to *do something*.

Budgets in the UK are sacrosanct. No one takes governments to court over budgets. But now financial planning was not above the law and the austerity review was a classic case. Government departments were warned by the women's minister, Theresa May, that they risked successful legal challenge.

Questions were asked in the House of Commons. The Treasury insisted that it had dutifully carried out an 'equality impact assessment'. Where? I asked the Treasury. Can we see it? It's on our website, said the Treasury. No it isn't, I said. Weeks later, the Treasury came back with a Freedom of Information reply: No, there had been no equality impact assessment. The legal challenge failed. Too late to do anything about it, said the judge. But a legal expert wondered, if not the budget then what? By 2012, five spending reviews later, the Treasury admitted that of nearly £15 billion raised, £11 billion came from women. And then the government announced that it was 'calling time' on equality impact assessments. Regressive redistribution away from women was rewarded by impunity.

LANDSCAPES OF THE FUTURE

The global is always also local: 'power geometry' defines the flows and movements, enablement and entrapment, between here, there and everywhere.[57] Gender in the hurtling economies of Asia and Latin America exemplifies Doreen Massey's concepts of power geometry and new forms of articulation of men's dominance over women.[58]

Towering Connections: South Korea

When the global financial system creaked and then tottered in 2008, digital-game designers in South Korea's NCsoft were launching Aion: the Tower of Eternity, an online multi-player game about power and subjugation, revolt and war, which was popular with both women and men. Unusually, NCsoft is known for its women web designers. South Korea is the most connected country in the world, a unique hub of online multi-player gaming among women and men.[59] Half of the South Koreans revel in social e-play, in imagined relationships in virtual castles and chasms called up on small screens. South Korea illuminates a seeming paradox: a bravura techno culture that is socially patriarchal. But there is no paradox: it simply belies the faith that somehow industrial innovation spontaneously yields socio-sexual emancipation.

A crew of heroic women attendants on South Korea's gleaming bullet trains mounted their own Aion, a 40-foot tower above the Korean railway offices in Seoul. They settled into a 60-day hunger strike, through violent rains and steaming heat, to broadcast their lament that women workers' 'lonely voices are not echoing in the society'.

Precariousness, the country's response to Asia's 1997 financial crisis, is a global strategy that transfers risk and resources away from the company to the worker.[60] About 70 per cent of South Korea's female labour market is precarious, a condition that provoked strikes, theatrical protests and hunger strikes against satellite and digital telecommunications giants that supply equipment to the world's leading manufacturers.[61]

South Korea's first woman shipyard welder, Kim Jin-suk, was a union representative at HHIC's Busan shipyard. In February 2011 she climbed 35 metres up to a metal cab on crane no. 85. Thus began the 'miracle on a precipice' protest.[62] This was her home for nearly a year. It wasn't just a crane, it was a sacred site—here union leader Kim Ju-ik had committed suicide during a strike against lay-offs in 2003.

Alone, often fearful of the dark nights and menacing police below, Kim Jin-suk communicated with the world by cell phone, and relied on comrades to send up food by bucket. She seemed to disappear from view until a poet, Song Kyung-dong, suggested a

Bus of Hope to gather solidarity round crane no. 85.[63] Police met the Hope Bus with water cannon and blockades. But they had not reckoned on TV star Kim Yeo-jin sho, who when arrested, alerted her 89,000 followers on Twitter. Instantly the Bus of Hope, the 'miracle on the precipice' and HHIC's industrial practices—including outsourcing to cheaper labour in the Phillipines—were national news.

Bus of Hope vigils gathered thousands round crane no. 85 every month until November 2011 when the company agreed to reinstate sacked workers and Kim Jin-suk decided she could return to the ground.[64]

South Korea has one of the OECD's lowest rates of women's labour market participation—and it is declining—and one of the highest gender pay gaps, 38 per cent. Precariousness produces gendered instability, powerlessness and dependence in a society in which three-quarters of married women do no paid work and are therefore absolutely dependent on men.

The country has one of the longest working and travel-to-work times in the world—men spend an average 77 minutes a day commuting. (The UK average is under 30 minutes.) Confucian capitalism renders South Korean men visitors to forlorn domesticity.[65] Since the 1980s, the country's fertility rate has been below the rate at which the country can reproduce itself; it is seemingly sterile and unsustainable.

Web designers in South Korea and Japan developed a novel aesthetic—the *cute*—that is the antithesis of the hypermuscular grotesques in the West's militaristic and gothic genres. The cute aesthetic or the 'techno cute'[66] became a universal, occidental–oriental, 'culturally friendly' visual vocabulary;[67] its 'play aesthetics' both cute and tough, more ambiguous than good vs evil, reached beyond boys to girls, women and men.[68]

In 2008 'the cute' was mobilized in South Korea's netizens' political iconography too. In May, schoolgirls ignited protests via the web against unsafe food and high tuition fees: 'mad cows, mad education'.[69] Dissent cascaded in mass candlelight picnics, pageants and vigils by girls, boys, men and women protesting against US beef imports, free trade, the education system, privatization and precariousness. The mascot was a rosy, unyielding girl with big eyes, holding a candle as big as her head.

The Eurasian wide eye is a specialism of Seoul's cosmetic surgeons. Students get a crease in their eyelids as coming-of-age presents. The city's international airport has a shuttle service for 'medical tourists'. Is it ethnic crossover, a *look* that is not just white and western but a global body?[70] Or, is it one of the ways in which the rich diversity of differently inscribed bodies is under threat from a hegemonic uniformity.[71]

Commodities in the homes and hands of consumers everywhere in the world are produced by global bodies that are fabricated not by cosmopolitanism but cosmetics. The utter ubiquity of cute avatars and global longings breach traditions of gender and generation:

'lonely voices' and 'candlelight girls' manage to surprise a society that is simultaneously the most 'connected' in the world and stuck in a hopeless sexual contract.

Murder City: Mexico

Claudia Ivette Gonzalez turned up late for her afternoon shift at a Lear Corporation factory on 10 October 2001. She was two or three minutes late. To punish her, Lear sent her off alone into one of the most dangerous zones in the world. It wasn't Afghanistan or Congo; it was Mexico's Ciudad Juárez, a boomtown between Chihuahua and Texas, a triumph of free trade and its accomplices, sexism and violence. She was found dead weeks later among the sexually mutilated bodies of several other women in a cotton field. Questioned about its responsibility for Gonzalez's safety, Lear Corporation insisted that her murder 'did not happen on Lear property'.[72]

Lear Corporation, headquartered in Michigan, located 19 of its 45 Mexico vehicle-components factories in Ciudad Juárez.

Founded by Spanish conquistadores in 1659, it is one of the industrial plantations along the US border, populated by more than a million people, thousands of whom work in *maquiladoras*. The majority live in *colonias*, typically made throughout Latin America by 'women, heroically building their own dwellings on unserviced peripheral land' out of plastic, cement blocks and scraps.[73]

Maquiladoras import materials and equipment from the US, tax-free, to manufacture goods for export back to the US, tariff-free. Hundreds of thousands of fast fingers and tired brains working 10- or 12-hour shifts transform millions of bits into components that share trade routes with drugs. One market is legal, the other isn't, but both oblige the insatiable tastes of the US market.

The biggest and baddest of these factory cities is Ciudad Juárez: in the six years after the declaration of war on drugs in 2006, an estimated 50,000 people had been killed. Ciudad Juárez trade union activist Verónica Leyva describes it as the definitive neoliberal city. Writer Charles Bowden calls it 'a laboratory for free-trade ideas' with 'nothing on the horizon that promises social peace'.[74] Violent democracy is crystallized here.[75] Mexico's public assets privatized, trade freed up by North American Free Trade Agreement (NAFTA) and *la frontera* militarized by the war against drugs. Crime is a variant of patriarchal political economy organized by secretive and sexually segregated hierarchies. In the borderlands, children, men—mayors, attorneys, journalists, bystanders and witnesses—are murdered. And women are murdered because they are women.

The city became synonymous with 'femicide': hundreds of women were murdered and mutilated and 3,000 disappeared. Memorials were posted on billboards, shop windows and walls. In 2002, Gonzalez's mother Josefina and feminist campaigners installed a memorial on that deadly cotton field, where they found the dress and shoes she had been wearing on the last day of her life; hair yanked from a woman's head; and a pair of overalls.

During a long campaign for justice, violent harassment forced one of the women's families to seek asylum in the US—it was granted. Finally, in 2009, the state was called to account at the Inter-American Court of Human Rights. It ruled that Mexico's police and security system encouraged 'an environment of impunity' and promoted 'the repetition of acts of violence in general'.[76] Together, congregations of men—capitalist corporations, drugs cartels, street bandits, the military, the police and politicians—made Ciudad Juárez a terminal kind of place.

Killing Fields: *India's Modernity*

India gasped. It was confronted by the worst of itself when a young woman died after being raped and eviscerated, while her friend was knocked out, on a bus in New Delhi. They were on their way home after seeing *Life of Pi* at the cinema. She came to be known as Braveheart. Her father Badhri Singh, a loader at Delhi airport, had sold his land to pay for her college education. After her death he revealed her name in her honour: Jyoti Singh Pandey.

Her brief survival, her longing to live, her friend's testimony about her heroic resistance, their naked bodies dumped in the street, police jurisdictional squabbles and an impoverished health service detonated mass protests about the *deadly* consequences of India's sexism.

This was unprecedented: India was not only talking about the death-by-rape of a working-class woman, it couldn't stop talking.[77] The world couldn't stop talking—it was a unique moment in human history.

India gasped in 2012 when Bollywood star Aamir Khan introduced three women to an estimated audience of 400 million. They were watching his debut television series *Satyamev Jayate*—primarily in Hindi and simulcast in half a dozen Indian languages, including English. The three women had been beaten, forced to abort foetuses or punished after giving birth to girls.

They were not women from poor, primitive hinterlands. One of them, Mitu Khurana, was a Delhi paediatrician. Her parents were doctors, her husband a surgeon, her in-laws academics. Her husband and his family vilified her and threw her out after she refused an ultrasound sex-determination test and gave birth to twin girls.

Khan lent his resources and reputation to a series of scalding investigations into Indian society in front of a live audience that often seemed wide-eyed with shock and sympathy. Indians had never seen anything like this, the press commented.

Femicide had been an open secret in India for a century, since the census began. The women's testimony broadcast prenatal sex selection and preference for male children that had first been exposed by feminists in the 1980s. This 'unexpected masculinization' of the population is a patriarchal phenomenon 'never before recorded in demographic history' that, population expert Christophe Z. Guilmoto predicts, will shape gender, generation and social welfare, violence and migration in the twenty-first century.[78]

Asia, the most economically dynamic region of the world, home to almost half the world's population, deprives the world of almost 170 million girls.

The 2011 census revealed that for every 1,000 baby boys in India there are only 914 baby girls. The richest northern states are the worst (they also have the lowest literacy rates for girls): in parts of Haryana and Punjab, the ratio is below 800 girls per 1,000 boys. And in some districts of Haryana the ratio is lower than 400 girls per 1,000 boys.[79]

Feminist campaigners alerted the government to clinics advertising ultrasound and sex selection in the 1980s and got the practice banned. To no avail. Impunity prevails. Prenatal sex selection, 'man-made high tech sexism',[80] accelerates the phenomenon disclosed by Amartya Sen's pioneering audit: at the end of the twentieth century, 'a great many more than a hundred million women are simply not

41

there' because of neglect and disease.[81] The presumption that Asia's industrial surge and neoliberal free market would emancipate women is nowhere more pitilessly exposed than by the region's foeticide compounded by femicide.

Villages and towns are bereft of women. But women do not profit from scarcity. Men buy women from poorer states. Re-domestication, prostitution, trafficking and violence beckon in what Guilmoto calls the 'new demographic regime of gender discrimination'.[82]

This business of killing girls and women is not the atavistic relic of patriarchal tradition; it is roused by the pleasures of mastery and renewed by defiance of daughters' rights to land, resources and autonomy.

The egalitarianism promised in India's constitution was extinguished by its historic compromise between secular modernity and ethnic/religious power over personal life—a proxy for patriarchal custodians of clan, caste, virtue and property.[83]

Men's *khap panchayat*s, an ancient, unelected mode of communal administration, maintain 'a largely regressive and parallel law enforcement agency' deploying community boycotts, exile, kidnap and killing 'in the name of brotherhood and honour'.[84] These traditionalists are 'radical', however, in their rejection of the rule of law, leaving government, judiciary and law enforcement 'slumped in defeat'.[85]

In 2010, in a middle-class suburb of New Delhi, police pulled out the body of a call centre worker, Kuldeep Singh, from a car; two bullets had killed him. Two bullets had killed his wife Monica and her cousin Shobha. Kuldeep and Monica had married without parental consent.

The bullets were fired by the women's brothers, cousins and friends from their old homestead, Wazirpur, a prosperous, formerly farming village near New Delhi, where property was made valuable by industrialization and proximity to the metropolis. 'Well done,' said family and neighbours.[86]

The first time an Indian court convicted assailants and ordered capital punishment in an honour killing case was in 2010—after nearly three years, 50 court hearings and evidence from 41 witnesses.[87] Manoj ran an electrical repair shop and Babli was a student. The khap panchayat mandated their killing. The couple sought police protection and fled. They were ambushed by Manoj's relatives and gunned down in 2007.

Manoj's mother and sister, supported by the All India Democratic Women's Association (AIDWA), campaigned for a criminal trial.[88] Five of Babli's relatives were found guilty of murder and a local *khap panchayat* leader was found guilty of conspiracy.

India's patriarchs were losing their mandate; they were scandalized. The judge herself, Vani Gopal Sharma, received death threats. Thousands of the *khap* leader's brethren gathered and demanded an appeal. Women took to the streets proclaiming 'no honour in killing' and condemning the 'ugly nexus between *khap* leaders, police and local politicians'.[89]

In honour and shame societies, argues human rights lawyer Ravi Kant, controlling women is paramount, since to control land, property and capital the brotherhood must control women.[90]

So, the diktats of the *khap panchayat*s do not wither, they multiply in response to insubordination by women and men.

India entered the twenty-first century still a largely rural economy. But fewer than 10 per cent of female offspring inherited land and even fewer had any control over it. Daughters are denied their property.[91] Men refuse to share the land with their mothers or sisters.[92] Only in 2005, as a result of adroit feminist activism, was equal right to inherit property between sons and daughters secured in the Hindu Succession Act.

Though India's homicide rate declines, that of dowry deaths rises. They account for more than half of all femicides.[93] Dowries function as a 'pre-mortem' pay-off.[94] The husband's family gets the dowry. The brothers get the land. They patrol their sisters—'girls choosing their own partners must be stopped at all costs'—and when they fail, the brotherhood 'pull triggers, raise axes and jab knives to set their sisters right': a mania is driven by 'power, patriarchy and property'.[95] This malign trinity, nesting in ancient caste and communal hierarchies, was re-invigorated by India's rush to industrialization and neoliberalism in the 1990s. By the second decade of the twenty-first century, the history of the global debt crisis repeated itself in India: fiscal crisis, flight of foreign capital and in 2013, collapsing currency.

Capital is transforming land and labour—and the life expectancy of female foetuses and girls. The fertile soils of Haryana and Punjab—India's 'bread basket'—were grabbed for state-sponsored development zones. Joint ventures by the governments of India and Japan mapped an industrialized arc from Delhi to Mumbai. Some of the richest

companies in the world were involved, from
India's Reliance and Tata, US' Monsanto to
Japan's Suzuki and Toyota. One-quarter of
Suzuki's revenue comes from India.

Economic strategy has increased productivity and raised millions from poverty. But
desperation ricochets across India—one-
quarter of a million farmers have committed
suicide since 1995.[96] Although the GDP
hit an all-time high, India is a model of what
Jayati Ghosh calls 'jobless growth': the economy grows but employment shrinks.[97]

India was not feminized by globalization,
insists Ghosh, rather, its labour market was
de-feminized. Women's share of the labour
market dived from almost half to below a
quarter, and the gender pay gap increased in
every category.[98] Microbanking, hailed as a
boon to women, represents less than 1 per
cent of credit. Women hold only 20 per cent
of deposit accounts. Only 15 per cent of
India's women actually receive pay. Where
are the women workers? Millions of them
toil in the informal economy. Much if not

most of women's work is uncounted and unpaid, a 'material articulation' of patriarchal domination.[99]

Among the G20 industrialized countries, India is the worst place for a woman.[100] Asia is the 'most globalized and economically dynamic region of the world' where patriarchy is not an epiphenomenon, argues Ghosh, it is 'fundamental to the capital accumulation process itself'.[101]

Equality in Reverse: China

Nowhere is the making of gender, and the gendered making of twenty-first-century modernity, more vividly *explicit* in the national narrative than in China.[102] After the 1949 communist revolution, the state sponsored equality as an index of its modernity. Millions of suffering women became partners in a great modernizing mission: they breathed revolutionary optimism and became icons of China's modernity, as rosy, brave, warm-hearted heroines ascending pylons, raising flags and driving tractors.

Millions survived famine and exhaustion. They gave up sleep to make clothes, soothe babies, nurse relatives, feed households while labouring, like men, for wages and sometimes, just for love of the new times.[103] New men did not match new women, however. So, women were already experts in the limits of the equality paradigm when China and the West opened their doors to each other at the end of the 1970s and China participated in the creation of the new world order.

Now the people were convened in a new narrative: liberation from socialism[104] promised a return to Confucian values and natural genders hidden by a supposedly asexual socialism, a historical transgression; femininity was spun as sexualized and subaltern.[105]

Selective amnesia became a weapon to 'take out' memories of women's movements, women's histories as political agents, women's insights into the synergy of sexual politics, state formation and national civilization. 'Radicalising questions' about how modernity is imagined[106] and about the salience of gender to structures of states and ideologies of civilization are erased in swooning celebration of China's epochal transition.[107]

Why, when China's state could release 200 million from poverty, did it have to privilege men, roll back welfare, make migrants into floaters and privatize childcare? Why do it *that* way?

Three decades of capitalism dragged women's relative participation in the labour market down, pensions down, access to public childcare down and the gender pay gap up.

Millions of women rushed out of subsistence work to the coastal factory campuses and into both emancipation and exploitation. The once (relatively) narrow gender pay gap widened: women's average earnings dropped from 86 per cent of men's in 1988 to 67 per cent (50 per cent for rural women) in 2011.[108] Before the transition, parenthood had little impact on pay but by the twenty-first century, the motherhood penalty soared to 40 per cent.[109]

The private and foreign sector propelled income inequality fast and fiercely. In China inequality grew faster and deeper than in any other transition country. China 'might well be the mother of all redistributions'.[110]

Formerly, enterprises provided childcare, now they don't—a mighty redistribution to men and capital. Only one-third of employed mothers have access to formal childcare.[111] In mass migrations millions of parents are separated from their children— nearly one-third of rural children are 'the left behind'.[112] Reciprocity, yearning and loss stretch across years and thousands of miles.[113]

The National Population and Family Planning Commission (NPFPC) estimates that two-thirds of migrant workers are without access to welfare. Shenzhen exemplifies the transition. The Pearl River Delta conurbation is twice the size of Los Angeles. Within 30 years, its skies changed from clean to dirty, its landscape from rice fields to skyscrapers and factories. Typically, half of the migrant workers do not have proper contracts, do not get regular pay and two-thirds never get days off.

A jewel of industrial innovation is Foxconn, China's biggest components exporter. Its factory estates in Shenzhen are home to 300,000 people. The story of China's rise is also the Foxconn story—and the story, therefore, of Apple, Nokia, Dell, Hewlett Packard, Sony and the world's leading brands of computers, phones and gizmos in general. Foxconn is also a target for consumer–worker solidarity that shames Apple, the most successful corporation on the planet, for complicity in hyper-exploitation.[114]

Foxconn boasts, we 'provided dormitories and cafeterias and everything; even laundries'. Not quite everything. The right to organize? Childcare? Scan the PR images of Foxconn's Shenzhen campus and there is a landscape eerily empty of children. It is a monument to masculinist economics and militaristic management that promises 'everything' except liveable social space.

The velocity of inequality in China provokes thousands of protests: land grabs resisted by flanks of elderly women who discombobulates the authorities; strikes and nuanced 'protest repertoires' of sleep-ins, go-slows, walks and 'sightseeing' perambulations.[115] The government implicitly acknowledged their impact by shifting rhetoric from growth towards social harmony.[116]

But state-sponsored capitalism and revived Confucianism ensure that for now, 'the mother of all redistributions' is China's contribution to the new neopatriarchal settlement.

SPACE AND VIOLENCE

Now I want to change the register, to move from economy and exploitation to power, violence and sex: the terrain of bodies.

Feminism is never only concerned with economies, exploitation and equality—it melts orthodox conceptions of power. Power is not just about resources, roles and rights.

Feminist political scientist Iris Marion Young cautions that power isn't a thing, a possession, it is a relationship: power infuses everyday life and the very making of human subjects and subjectivities. Patriarchal power relationships polarize notions of masculinities and femininities.

Power works through dominion and dependence and although power may be hegemonic it is never absolute. It is lived in cultures and actions, through censure, control and consent.

Masculinities are conferred with the capability and the crafts of violence; violence in general and against women, in particular, is spectacularly refreshed in the new social spaces created by the world wide web. I've learnt from young men serving long or life sentences in prison about the logic of menace, violence and terror for mastery; and its collateral, the productivity and pleasure of pain: the suffering of others and in themselves the soothing biochemistry of shock.

In patriarchies a woman 'lives her body as object as well as subject'; bodies restlessly submit to a kind of 'self-surveillance' that is both a form of agency and subordination, a kind of 'obedience';[117] Patriarchies solicit women's subordination and participation, and of course seek women's consent.

The Wire *and* The City of God

The US television series *The Wire* (2002–08) is an allegory of cities living their very death, excited and wounded by money, menace and violence. Nothing in US television fiction was so large, ambitious and so black, gorgeously black. *The Wire* is where picaresque roguery meets gothic melancholia.

Omar Devone Little is a gay gangsta whose allure lies in his wit, beauty and eloquent brutality; his main men are his lovers and, for a while, he enlists a couple of women shooters who are also glamorous and gay. They are *not* criminal archetypes—they are a beautiful fiction. Omar's death, however, is no fairy tale; it is consistent with life expectancy in the backyards of neoliberalism.

If *The Wire* is a portrait of dystopian decline, Paulo Lins' 1997 novel *The City of God* (later a film) is a pitiless dramatization of ungoverned growth. Lins' novel came out of his work with the radical anthropologist Alba Zaluar in Rio de Janeiro. She proposes that toxic locales are created by rapid unplanned urbanization, inequality and symbiosis between legal and illegal economic systems, between crime and hypermasculinities.

Crime and violence are thoroughly gendered contexts and 'resources' in the making of masculinity as both mastery and martyrdom. Young men stake out territory that may be only the circumference of a street corner but they assert control through chaos, a kind of insurgency that is freed up when the local state is diminished and when financial systems limit democratic institutions' ability to manage social space.[118]

Geographies of violence make spectacular appearances in the neoliberal, neo-patriarchal era. For every great city there is a slum or a war zone that the world's great places depend upon and determine.[119] Megacities are monuments not only to towering capital but also to everyday life, escape and violence, rape and pillage *somewhere* or the other.

For millions of people, new times and new democracies mean insecurity, violence and death, with 'states, social elites, and subalterns employing violence' as mechanisms of control or of coping with the consequences of neoliberal policies. Violence is not evidence of failure but of a way of functioning.[120]

Violence splatters everyday life. The foot soldiers, typically poor boys, are disciplined and doomed. Rage at the state's failure to ensure citizens' safety encourages lethal retribution. Lynching becomes a form of 'flexible justice', police take the law into their own hands and poor boys become, literally, 'killables'.[121]

Rougher Methods

Armed conflicts proliferate. When British diplomat Robert Cooper mentored UK prime minister Tony Blair's foreign policy he ventured a theory that the 'death of imperialism' releases failed, premodern states to loiter with intent on the threshold of the West. He advocated a 'New Imperialism' deploying 'the rougher methods of an earlier era—force, pre-emptive attack and deception; whatever is necessary' to overpower the West's enemies. The 'New Imperialism' leases violence to *men*—warlords, mercenaries, auxiliaries, security corporations, religious fundamentalists, vigilantes, princes and patriarchs almost anywhere. Cooper was no scary neoconservative: he wrote this manifesto in the liberal *Observer* on 7 April 2002.[122]

Modern warfare is a riot of insurgencies and counterinsurgencies,[123] rupturing distinctions between public and private, soldier and civilian. A priority for militarism, writes Mary Kaldor, is how violent masculinities are made and maintained. The product is terror, rape, plunder and predatory 'trade' and smuggling. Violations of human rights are not side effects but the decisive methodology.[124]

Wars are neither noble nor humanitarian; they create a kind of purgatory into which men hurl their bodies, bullets, toxic spray, heavy metal and now remote missiles into the blood of others. Now the etiquette of war-making that was supposed to reserve the mayhem for men only is abandoned.

The nineteenth-century scramble for Africa, a scandal in the making of Western modernity,[125] is reprised in an armed rush for minerals prized in global markets. In the Democratic Republic of the Congo, five million people, mostly civilians, are estimated to have died from the armed conflict and its consequences—rape, pillage, disease and devastation—and millions more displaced.[126]

'Humanitarian imperialism' left Afghanistan the worst place in the world for a woman.[127] During the 'humanitarian' emancipation of Iraq two-thirds of the dead were civilians. The International Red Cross regularly reported abuse 'tantamount to torture'.[128] The new Iraq's constitution reinstated the power of the clerics and 'wider permissive brutalising of women's lives [. . .] permeates the new Iraq in its entirety'.[130]

Sexism became a novel resource in the army—women were enlisted to sexually humiliate male detainees and women detainees were, more predictably, sexually abused by men. Within the US military, sexual abuse and harassment threatened women—many of whom escaped abusive homes—who comprised 15 per cent of US active duty personnel.[130]

The war against drugs in Central America is, of course, sponsored by the major cocaine consumer and banker: the US itself. While murder rates decline in Europe and Asia, they rise in the Americas. South America is saturated with guns; 74 per cent of its homicides involve firearms.[131] Dangerousness and the elusiveness of justice have come to be known as *the impunity*.[132]

Crime and proliferating armed conflicts can be seen as a neoliberal paradigm: free trade unfettered by social responsibility, organized by unaccountable fraternities of police, militias and mafia.

The most violent regions of the world are associated with the privatization of the public sector, policing and security.[133] They become not so much no-man's-lands as man's lands where impunity prevails.

Militarism, crime and violence are contexts for doing or making masculinity.[134] Unsafe cities and war zones multiply the arenas for rape and repudiation of women. Violence is not a sign of primitive masculinity or the collapse of civilization; it is its hardened heart.

SEX AND VIOLENCE

When feminism is repudiated, inequalities stretch and crimes against women attract impunity; femininities are taken to extremes and empowerment is invested in the body and in men: fortunes are made from enhancing or shrinking bosoms, lips, skin; blood is shed over the veil—a geopolitical fetish that draws attention to the thing that must not be seen, the body that is so dangerously desired.

The built body and the masked body are oddly united in one thing: a pessimistic engagement with masculinity. It is represented as a force to be aroused and managed, or feared and managed—but not changed.

Feminist sexual politics causes calumny when it discloses the scale and structures of intimate oppression. It is diagnosed as a politics of 'victimhood' and its appeal to state and society to take the side of women, to contemplate intimate oppression is traduced as 'injury as identity', fixing women in subordination, as dodging the hard politics of redistribution for the soft option of recognition, as bleating on and on.[135]

Certainly, sexual politics is risky politics—harm and humiliation are hard to hear, rapport is hazardous[136]—but there has never been feminism without it. The following vignettes take us into terrain created by feminism but where there is no feminist consensus.

Jordan and the Self-Made Woman

Humans landed on the moon; the richest country in the world was about to lose a war with one of the poorest; Dusty Springfield and Stevie Wonder both had three hit records; half a million people converged at the Woodstock Festival; and the UK Parliament passed the Equal Pay Act.

It was 1969—the year Australian media mogul Rupert Murdoch acquired the *Sun* and launched a counter-revolutionary assault on women in particular and British democracy in general. The *Sun* made scurrility an art form. Its ethos was sex, sensation and sport.[137] In 1970, the women's liberation movement landed in the UK and the *Sun*'s buccaneering sexism answered with a taunt—Page 3. It entered British discourse: it meant the daily nude, the emblem of the *Sun*'s pride in 'giving the public what they want'.[138] But it was never innocent—a passive or reciprocal relationship to ready-made readers. It did not so much reflect the public as create a manly, misanthropic and patriotic public.

The paper became the jewel in a media empire that held parliamentary parties in its fearful thrall until 2012 when Murdoch's News International was disgraced for cascading corruption—it had thoroughly penetrated the police, illegally hacked into thousands of private telephones, created a 'network of corrupted public officials' in 'strategic places across public life'.[139]

Overheated sexism boiled the blood of its populist genius. The paper organized the male gaze and it disorganized women. It invited millions of men to open up hitherto secret pleasures to the women and children they lived with. Page 3 lay around on kitchen tables, sofas, cabs, canteens and toilets, telling everyone what women were for, putting women in their place, to procure the demanding, desiring gaze of the *Sun*'s public.

One such woman was Katie Price, a teenager also known as Jordan, who appeared in the *Sun* in the 1990s until the paper's 'natural bodies' policy excluded women who had surgically enhanced theirs. But Jordan prospered, her bosom getting variously bigger and smaller. Her built body epitomized the parable of the self-made woman. She became a reality-television 'celebrity' who raised bewitching blether to new heights in her own un/reality series; she branded herself, made almost £3 million by selling exclusive access to her weddings and became a best-selling author who neither wrote nor read her own books.[140]

Here a confession is called for: I didn't register her significance until I saw a long queue—a very long queue—of women outside a bookshop in Manchester for a Katie Price book-signing, the first of her many autobiographies.

The body that began its public life as a sexual object had apparently became a subject;[141] the body that was exposed to elicit men's desire became a spectacle for women: they would bear witness to the shaving, plucking, dyeing, dieting, stuffing, suffering and the sheer stamina that are the process of the production of such a woman.

Her CV became a cliché of 'erotic capital', of banality and burlesque chutzpah. Her reputation as that rare phenomenon, a woman at ease with herself, whose body carried 'neither vanity nor insecurity',[142] was all propaganda of course. She couldn't leave that body alone.

Publishing gave birth to new genres of niche sexism: pornography, 'probably the number-one moneymaker on the web'[143] and the proliferation of celebrity and lifestyle magazines targeting women as spectators and critics of women's bodies. Katie launched her own magazine in 2011—*Katie, My Magazine*— its 115 pages crowded with 124 pictures of herself.

Celebrity, ubiquity, wealth could not, however, overcome the sex and class limits of this material girl's body and its audience. Maddy Coy and Maria Garner reckon that though she 'accumulated economic capital she was socially and culturally bankrupt'.[144] Class will out: Price couldn't pass, she could never join the elite—though an accomplished horsewoman, she could never get into Cartier's annual polo party.

Being seen has never given women social power. Celebrity lives by different lore from the mantra bequeathed by George III to the monarchy: Be seen, above all be seen. If display serviced the cult of monarchy as supremacy and sovereignty, celebrity merely serviced sexism.

The Veiled Body

Images of veiled women were raising record prices and drawing record audiences in the art galleries of France at the very time in the 2000s when real-life veiled women were being vilified and banned from public life. The irony is manifest in a portrait: *Femme circassienne voilée*, painted in 1876 by the French Orientalist artist Jean-Léon Gérôme. It raised more than £2 million at Christie's auction house in 2007 when it was bought by oil-rich Qatar, whose royal princelings create a realm of conspicuous consumption—of gold, football clubs and, it seems, white men's fantasies in Orientalist art. Qatar's women, meanwhile, may only appear in public veiled from head to foot.

In 2010, France passed a law against women covering their faces in public and *Femme circassienne voilée* adorned the walls of the Musée d'Orsay. She was part of an international exhibition reviving the reputation of Orientalism—a booming genre during the French conquest of Africa, later discredited by anti-colonialist and feminist critiques of Orientalism as the imperial, patriarchal gaze, flagrant and wide-eyed.[145]

Gérôme's fantasy woman is 'black' but appears 'white', she is less *voilée* than décolleté: her scant black veil laces her curls and her sombre face, and sweeps round her shoulders almost disclosing a white bosom. In the gallery she keeps company with Gérôme's fictions—of harems, bath houses, mosques and slave markets—populated not by women but by nudes, for the peeping, penetrating eye of imperial men.

In French politics, however, the veil and the niqab, though scarcely present, were interpreted not as seduction but as a sign of subordination on the one hand and as provocation and aggression on the other— an affront to the spirit of citizenship and the French republic.[146]

Historian Joan Wallach Scott tracks the history of the veil as a crisis for French colonialists, driven to distraction by Arabs who 'elude us' because they 'conceal their women from our gaze'.[147] During Algeria's national liberation struggle, women concealed the means of resistance, weapons historically denied to them. The veil and the burqa signify both subjugation and an insurgent's shield.

The veil, the chador, the burqa and the hijab surface in the twenty-first century as an effect of anxiety about national identities and geopolitics that are refracted through the bodies of women.[148]

It is argued by some that Muslim women's agency, religious passion and resistance can be announced by covering themselves.[149] Feminist writer and activist Rahila Gupta's unyielding riposte is that 'this is a cloth that comes soaked in blood.' It never shields women from risk, 'women get raped even when they are covered from head to foot.'[150]

The question: to be nude or to be covered is a proxy for other agendas—national liberation, national identity, national security and modernity. Like the nude, the veiled woman is thoroughly eroticized—covering is predicated on masculinity as predatory. Her veil is not the livery of liberation, it is the radical performance of pessimism.

The Bed and the Gallery

Tracey Emin became a quixotic eminence in her generation of Brit artists. She brings into vision a body's life story that is closeted by art, by Page 3 and pornography, and by the veil: abused girlhood, rape, abortion, disrespect and war. Her stories appear in neon, appliqué, embroidery, photography and film, and in the scratched, sketched eloquence of a distraught body: her own.

In one of the founding texts of British feminism in the 1970s, John Berger wrote that to be naked is to be oneself while to be nude is to be seen naked but not recognized for oneself; the nude's purpose is to service desire in spectator-owner, not to have her own.[151] Emin's naked woman—herself—is not a nude. Emin doesn't do nudes. She doesn't expose herself so much as disclose herself. Her art bears witness, it is an argument; it invites empathy and pleasure and aching melancholia.

Self-portrait is her strategy of disclosure about what it means to be in a woman's body. She 'speaks back through her art', argues Rosemary Betterton, it is a 'means of resistance against former silencing'.[152] She herself stands between the object—the art—and the spectator, and often surrounds these *objets d'art* with text that is sometimes part of the image, sometimes her diary, a scribble,

appliqué or neon, all of it expressing a
commitment to intelligibility in her art and
candid contemplation of the life that produces it:[153]

> please—dose (sic) not necessarily
> mean please fuck me
> it means please stop . . .
> I'd rather masturbate any day than
> break someone's heart.

This autobiographical art attracts pas-
sionate commentary, from pleasure and
empathy to huffy impatience with the 'personal' in her project, and disappointment
with her periodic lack of sympathy with
other women's bruised bodies.[154] The argument is also society's argument with itself
about representations of sex, power, pleasure and pain: about both her art *as art* and
the sexual politics that animates it; as if
Emin's return to the site of her body, simultaneously pleasure-seeking and harmed, is
mentally disordered; as if working with the
material she knows—herself—is feeble; as if
autobiography is an exhausted genre; as

if her home town of Margate, her body and popular culture—all her territory—are worthless.

(Do these grumblers say of Edgar Degas—enough with the legs and the tutus? Or of Goya or Giotto—too much grief, or of Lucien Freud's boiled bodies—don't they all look the same?)

Though a hygienic sniff greeted the presumed sluttishness of *My Bed* when it appeared in 1998 at the Tate Gallery, it attracted a rush of spectators: they were interested in that bed, some of them loved that bed—the cheek of it in an art gallery, a bed strewn with the detritus of everyday life, a bed without a naked woman.

That *mise en scène* was fastidiously assembled: she didn't fall out of her bed, she designed it. Her art doesn't show dysfunction, it defies the shame that, like fear, demobilizes women whatever they wear, wherever they live, and offers an 'ethical riposte' to what art licenses men to do to women.

73

These silhouettes are united by one thing: the stories women's bodies tell us about some men, lots of men, and what they want to do to women.

Rape and Impunity

Roman Polanski was not coy: he proclaimed his desire to 'fuck young girls'. After the celebrated film director was charged in 1977 with drugging, raping and sodomizing a 13-year-old girl in Hollywood, he fled to the welcome embrace of 'very grown up' France and at a Cannes press conference yelled, 'I will say again, once and for all, I love very young girls.'[155] He boasted to British writer Martin Amis, 'Judges want to fuck young girls. Juries want to fuck young girls—everyone wants to.'

'No,' Amis replied, 'not everyone.'[156]

Sulphurous confusion about rape and sexual abuse of children, and the meaning—and crucially context—of consent flared three decades later when the US sought Polanski's extradition in 2009. Comic star

Whoopi Goldberg ventured that the case was not clear-cut, it was not 'rape-rape' and so 'rape-rape' joined the notion of 'real rape' in the lexicon of denial.

The Polanski debate was swiftly followed by brouhaha in grown-up France itself. In 2011, the International Monetary Fund (IMF) chief, Dominique Strauss-Kahn, a notorious libertine, was accused by New York hotel worker Nafissatou Diallo of attempted rape. DNA tests confirmed Strauss-Kahn's semen on her clothing and in the room. Yes, there had been sex, Strauss-Kahn admitted, but it was consensual. Many people regarded the scandal as a set-up, a conspiracy against France, until French women added their own allegations. The seducer now appeared as predator. By 2012 police implicated Strauss-Kahn in a prostitution conspiracy and multiple perpetrator rape: now he was *persona non grata*.[157]

Prostitution, too, was becoming unwelcome in France. Suspected pimps operating classy clubs round the Champs-Elysées were

put under police surveillance. Police inter-
viewed 18 young women and several clients,
including some of the country's most celebrated footballers. The case became known
as 'birthdaygate': France's star footballer
Franck Ribéry had flown 16-year-old Zahia
Dehar to Germany as a birthday present to
himself.

These cases were a crisis for French culture: in 2011 the National Assembly declared
that it aspired to 'a society without prostitution'. Elements of the French elite didn't
give up. The kitsch count of French fashion,
Karl Lagerfeld, threw his fingerless studded
leather gauntlet at 'political correctness' and
hailed Zahia as an exemplar of the courte-
san, 'a purely French tradition that the whole
world admired'.[158]

Zahia was made. Sponsored by an
anonymous wealthy man, installed in a pala-
tial apartment lined with mirrors, a retro
bordello, she was given a fashion business
with her own designers and promoters and a
show at the Paris Couture Fashion Week, a

collage of sex-shop undies masquerading as lingerie.

In her new incarnation she reprised her old pastiche persona of babydoll or Barbie in 'erotic scenes' on her website. She attracted 'exclusive' interviews in *Paris Match* and *Libération*, which describe her variously as a bird fallen from a nest, an orphan, a fairy, a rags-to-riches Cinderella. Everything about Zahia's history as a middle-class, North African teenager, hanging around the Champs-Elysées, bought by men, is erased in her image, bleached out, like a geisha, who seemed animated only when she looked at herself, the ingénue made interesting by a little degradation.[159]

She received Lagerfeld's benediction. He produced her show's lookbook (catalogue) and proclaimed prostitution as a suitable profession: 'Big courtesans have a big future,' he reportedly said. But no, she insisted, she was not a prostitute, it was men who propositioned her: 'They proposed, I disposed.' She'd done it for the money: 'Anyone can do

it from time to time.' Nor was she a 'sex sym-
bol' she said. 'Me? I don't know what I am
exactly, it is other people who know.'[160]

Making Capital out of It

Sex work is perhaps feminism's most fissile
material—one of those themes, like euthana-
sia, capital punishment, child abuse, the European Union, smoking—that slices through
political alignments. Unlikely protagonists
find themselves in shared discursive space.[161]
Add conservative backlash, mass migration,
Internet innovation and it ferments anew as
wild problematics.[162]

The ideology of the market prevails as a
metaphor for life and the theory of 'erotic
capital' appears as a reassuring vindication
of femininity as a mission to arouse, to elicit
desire and exact a price.[163] Its fluffy allure is
in the coupling of eros and economy and the
intimation that the erotic isn't relational, it's
just a resource. 'Erotic capital' belongs to a
medley of definitions of 'sex work' that flirt
with common sense and seek deliverance

from what is perceived to be *moral* puri-
tanism and feminist outrage. The hyperbole
of capitalism itself is enlisted: 'Indian Sex
Workers are a Shining Example of Women's
Empowerment';[164] Sex workers 'object to
being treated as symbols of oppression'.[165]
Sex trade, it is said, is simply selling and buying pleasure and leisure, as if the erotic is
fixed and universal, as if 'economy' is everything.[166] It is as if individuals are always only
accumulating and as if society is merely a mar-
ketplace. As if workers are not exploited or
oppressed. And so, the dangerous discovery
that in capitalism work is a social relationship
wrapped in domination and dispossession
evaporates.

Of course, anything that can be commod-
ified—including sex—can enter the circuit of
capital. But the thrill of Marx's *Manifesto* and
Capital is the critique of 'commodity fetishism'
and capitalism's reduction of power relations
between human beings into trade in things,
and of capitalism as a *social relationship* vested
simultaneously in commodities and control.

It is a system that struggles for hegemony, that masks its own contradictions and antagonisms and makes invisible—to women—that which demands visibility. Cultural theorist Stuart Hall cautions that Marx's 'somewhat problematic formulation' of the economy as 'determining in the last instance' gets to be interpreted as 'first, middle and last instance'.[167]

This tendency is exemplified by advocates of 'erotic capital' and 'sex work'; these terms slip into each other's arms and slink into straitened economic reductionism; they hush the torrential complexities, the risk, adventure, deception, fright and shame that are the lived life of sexual commerce.

The very repetitions and limits of the argument reveal the sheer difficulty—and necessity—of freeing up *sexual* politics from dour abstractions of labour power, capital and supply and demand.

This is a 'man question' that is typically framed as a 'woman question' predicated on women's economy, choice, autonomy, safety and virtue. Hence, for some, 'the extension of workers' rights to all those who sell sex should be a point of urgency for feminist activists.'[168] Men are exempted in 'the economy of erotic capital', as if men were not participants in a social relationship. Men possess only 'empty purchasing power', ventures writer Laurie Penny, they are 'almost entirely consumers, and almost entirely marginalised as individuals'.[169] This is not confirmed by what men themselves have to say about buying women.[170]

'Prostitution societies' from shogunate Japan, China and India, *quartier*s of 'carnal commerce' in Renaissance Europe and militarized encampments all over the world certainly tell us that women in patriarchies have tried to evade punishing, sequestered domesticity and poverty to muster an income and relative autonomy in specialized sex zones.[171] These zones' *raison d'être* has not been the empowerment of women, however, but the sovereignty of men, from popes to princes.

Sex work only exists insofar as sexism exists. The product may be sex, but it is always also sexism. It is an opportunity for men to be masters.[172] Political scientist Carole Pateman clarifies the problem: in capitalism labour power is 'an abstraction' and owners and buyers only *appear* to buy labour power. Actually, they obtain 'the right of command over workers' and 'their capacities'.[173]

For almost a century, the ILO has intervened with governments, agents, police and individuals to enforce international laws and human rights protocols. In 2008, it published the first global estimate of the number of people held in forced labour: more than 12 million, over 40 per cent of them sexually exploited. By 2012, the ILO estimate topped 20 million persons whose employers bask in almost universal impunity.[174] 'Impunity is a major root cause of trafficking,' says the ILO.[175] And it is getting worse—the rise of state regulation of 'labour providers' is being 'reversed' and private cross-border recruiters profit from weak national scrutiny.[176] Thus, impunity and tighter immigration controls mean migrant workers and recruiters 'are willing to pay even higher prices to meet each other'.[177]

The notion of sex workers' rights as *workers'* rights, in contrast to *human* rights, crumbles in these contexts, where the most vulnerable 'have little to gain and a lot to lose' from informing on the exploiters. What takes her to them, what is the price of her dazed sorrows? What can 'choice' and 'rights' mean, therefore, to a girl snared by men who want to take control of her body?

What we know is that where sex work flourishes so does sexism.

Impunity

After the women's liberation movement established rape crisis centres in the early 1970s, and women were able to reinterpret and redistribute blame for sexual crime, alliances were made between survivors, women's services and professionals. These alliances challenged and changed ideologies and institutions, from policing to psycho-analysis, the law and public service. Rape and abuse could no longer be regarded as hapless excess or even envy but as strategies to humiliate and dominate.

Confronting intimate atrocities is treacherous politics; it has to withstand the perpetrators' power, the listeners' flood of fear, awe and disgust.[178] It has to overcome shame, strategic silence and retraction. The effort of telling and listening must be reciprocal; only if society's secrets become public knowledge can society know itself and change itself. But sexual assault and violence shows how the sovereignty of institutions and ideologies can be radically shaken *and* restabilized. Despite crests of new awareness of prevalence of rape and sexual abuse and their traumatic impact, no society in the world takes the side of women and children against the perpetrators.

Rape is unusual: in peacetime, most suspects are known to the victim but throughout the world most victims never get justice. Over 90 per cent of rape is never reported and 80 per cent of reported rape in the UK is not acted upon or the complaint is withdrawn. If victims are no longer disparaged by the police they are discouraged and dissuaded. Only half of the lamentable 14 per cent of cases that go to trial result in a conviction.

The largest victim study in the UK found that every year more women were reporting rape but the ratio of prosecution and conviction declined, reaching an all time low of 5.6 per cent in 2002 and thereafter hovering between 6 and 7 per cent.[179]

For the first time the Metropolitan Police delved into their own rape records to find out why. The evidence slumbering in the files was dynamite.[180] The vast majority of victims were in categories that made them vulnerable— they had been involved with the perpetrators or had mental-health histories or they had been drinking or they were young. So predators target women and girls who attract police pessimism.[181] The police were focused on the virtues of the victims as witnesses and not the tactics or histories of the perpetrators.[182] Yet, the Metropolitan Police chose to bury the evidence rather than share it or learn from it.[183]

What about the suspects? Another shock: one-quarter—including men who had not been traced or investigated—had records of violent offences.

Juries are reluctant to send men down but they also respond to law and evidence, 'the strongest direct evidence produces the highest conviction rates.'[184] Poor outcomes follow poor investigation.

The Metropolitan Police fielded the biggest team of specialist rape investigators in the world. After these revelations, surely, the police would do better: outcomes would improve. They didn't. Decades of scrutiny, controversy and historic law reform produced little or no improvement.[185] 'Procedural injustice' is replicated throughout the world.[186] That means 'impunity [. . .] for the vast majority of rapists'.[187]

In China and India, two cases of sexual violence detonated outrage about seemingly everything. Class, power, corruption, women's victimization and heroism converged in these societies' distressed sense of themselves.

Deng Yujiao was working in a hotel in Badong County as a pedicurist in 2009 when an enraged business official threw himself at her, waved wads of banknotes and threatened to 'smack her to death with money' after she refused to provide sexual services. Fighting him off, she stabbed him with her pedicure knife. When she was charged with murder, an Internet 'mass incident' gathered an estimated four million hits—against ostentatious inequality and lawless government and the fright of a woman.

After the horrific rape of the young woman in New Delhi who came to be known as Braveheart, India was angry; demonstrations spread in homage to the woman and in protest against political sclerosis and sexism. For the first time 'words like patriarchy [were] being discussed on the streets'.[188] Everything about the woman's life and death—her tenacity, the rapists' sadistic excess, the bystanders' indifference, the police sloth, the hospital's inadequacy—was an affront to the best of India. Had Braveheart died instantly and alone, her dumped body would have been just another naked nuisance.

Police and prosecutors are overwhelmed by the victim, dead or alive, as a problem. Nowhere in the world do the police quarry their capacious archives of sex crime to enhance collective consciousness.

Inevitably, it is the question of consent rather than the suspect's strategy and creation of context that animates the criminal justice system.[189] When cases rest on the question of consent they fail to distinguish 'between actual consent and the suspect's construction of consent, of yes,' as Betsy Stanko, the Metropolitan Police's director of research puts it. Consent cannot be given when it cannot be refused.[190] The political logic of rape is the defeat and dishonouring of victims; their selfhood is condemned, put to shame, and what awaits victims 'in the criminal justice system is a theatre of shame'.[191]

Impunity does not come from confusion. It is collusion. It is the impeachment of survivors. Doubt about 'real rape', 'rape-rape' or 'legitimate rape' is actually an argument about whether it matters—it is the semantics of deciding to not-know and not-care, it is taking the side of perpetrators. The most masculinized of public services, the judiciary, police and peacekeepers, do not take inspiration from the collective body of women: 'the scene of crime'.

Justice and Redress

Politically, the spaces between shame, righteous indignation, repair and redress are where we find ourselves. Justice that is confined to law and individual liability does not induce a sense of shared liability in popular culture. It does not censure sexism as the sponsor of sexual harm. It stifles the language of life and the effort of recovery from fright.[192]

What does justice mean to survivors of intimate oppression, whether virtual or visceral? What does democracy mean to women whose experience is scorned, who survive war between men, gangs, militias and states but who form no part of the decision-making that produces war or peace, life or death?[193]

It is shame and dishonour that render 'crimes of sexual domination so impervious to the formal remedies of the law' Judith Lewis Herman tells us. Honour is traditionally guarded by and for men. Forgiveness, a demand made of women, 'is giving up all hope of a better past'.[194]

What do recognition and redress mean in landscapes drenched by 'social suffering' where the unnoticed wit and heroism that makes up everyday life amid chronic violence is never regarded as a resource for politics?[195] Feminism's project is to bear witness to what Veena Das calls the 'choke and sting of experience'.[196]

Validation and vindication is not the reification of victimhood.[197] It is politically elusive but restorative—bringing honour in the justice system to victims of crimes of violence and sexual domination may seem modest', suggests Herman, but it is 'profoundly radical.'[198]

Impunity is a crisis of politics: it incubates pessimism about the means of making a difference and it reinstates the sovereignty of sexism.

In Conclusion

Global institutions no longer endorse men's power as *men*, but the world is being governed by a neopatriarchal and neoliberal matrix that assails—and provokes—feminism's renaissance. This is the new form of articulation of men's dominance over women—from sexual violence to human rights protocols and equality laws, budgets, time, money and care. A new sexual settlement is being made. But it is unsustainable.

If the history of feminism's first wave is the history of democracy in the making and the second wave a response to the sexism and the limits of democracy, then the emerging tidal crests confront the new matrix and demand an alternative to the sexist dominion of social spaces and democracies' disreputable decline.

The new historic settlement is sovereign but it is also shaky and contested. It is a fate from which we must save the world and ourselves.

Imagine men without violence. Imagine sex without violence. Imagine that men stop stealing our stuff—our time, our money and our bodies; imagine societies that share the costs of care, that share the costs of everything; that make cities fit for children; that renew rather than wreck and waste. This is women's liberation. It is do-able, reasonable and revolutionary.

To paraphrase from the *Manifesto of the Communist Party* once more:

> Feminism is already acknowledged by all powers to be itself a power; it is high time that feminism meets this myth of the 'Spectre of Feminism' with its own new manifestos.

Notes

1   Karl Marx, *Manifesto of the Communist Party* (Samuel Moore trans.) (New York: Cosimo Inc., 2009), p. 38.

2   See Judith Williamson, 'Sexism With an Alibi', *Guardian* (31 May 2003).

3   Suzanne Pullon Fitch and Roseann M. Mandziuk, *Sojourner Truth As Orator: Wit, Story, and Song* (Westport, CT: Greenwood Publishing Group, 1997), p. 125.

4   'Student Nonviolent Coordinating Committee Position Paper: Women in the Movement, November 1964', The Sixties Project website. Available at: http://www2.iath.virginia.edu/sixties/HTML_docs/Resources/Primary/Manifestos/SNCC_women.html (last accessed on 28 June 2013).

5   Contrary to the charges of Nancy Fraser in 'Feminism, Capitalism and the Cunning of History', *New Left Review* 56 (March–April 2009): 97–117, that feminism fell for a 'dangerous liaison', a 'perverse, subterranean, elective affinity' with neoliberal capitalism;

and Hester Eisenstein, *Feminism Seduced: How Global Elites Use Women's Labour and Ideas to Exploit the World* (Boulder, CO: Paradigm Publishers, 2009).

6   Sarah Fenstermaker and Candace West, *Doing Gender, Doing Difference: Inequality, Power and Institutional Change* (London: Routledge, 2002), p. 44; Ching Kwan Lee, *Gender and the South China Miracle: Two Worlds of Factory Women* (Berkeley: University of California Press, 1998), p. 31.

7   Candace West and Don H. Zimmerman, 'Doing Gender', *Gender and Society* 1(2) (June 1987): 125–51; Candace West and Don H. Zimmerman, 'Accounting for Doing Gender', *Gender and Society* 23 (February 2009): 112–22; Judith Butler, *Gender Trouble* (London: Routledge, 1990), p. 41.

8   Susan Himmelweit and Hilary Land, 'Reducing Gender Inequalities to Create a Sustainable Care System (October 2008), Joseph Rowntree Foundation website. Available at: http://www.jrf.org.uk/publications/reducing-gender-inequalities-create-sustainable-care-system (last accessed on 28 June 2013).

9   Ibid.

10 Equality and Human Rights Commission, *Sex and Power Report 2008* (London: EHRC, 2008).

11 See Amartya Sen, 'More than 100 Million Women Are Missing', *New York Review of Books* 37(20) (20 December 1990): 61–6.

12 I use the articulation here as outlined by Stuart Hall, as the form of connection between ideology/theory/discourses and social forces that may not be determined, absolute and essential, but which *can* make a unity of different elements; See Stuart Hall, *Critical Dialogues in Cultural Studies* (London: Routledge, 1996), pp. 115–42; See Ernesto Laclau and Chantal Mouffe, 'Hegemony and Socialist Strategy' (2nd edn, London: Verso, 2001).

13 See Viviana A. Zelizer, 'A Humbler Bonus', *Huffington Post* (31 January 2009). Available at: http://www.huffingtonpost.com/viviana-a-zelizer/a-humbler-bonus_b_162824.html (last accessed on 2 July 2013).

14 Aditya Chakrabortty, 'Britain Is Ruled by the Banks, For the Banks', *Guardian* (12 December 2011).

15 See Sarah Rutherford, 'Written Evidence to House of Commons Treasury Select Committee' (September 2009). Available at: http://-www.publications.parliament.uk/pa/cm2009-10/cmselect/cmtreasy/482/482we14.htm (last accessed on 2 July 2013).

16 The Treasury Select Committee was so alarmed that it organized hearings on sexism in the City in 2009.

17 See Deborah Hargreaves, 'It is Obscene for Bosses to Continue to Take Big Bonuses', *Guardian* (20 September 2012).

18 Federico Cocco 'Gender Pay Gap: How is Britain Faring?' Available at: http://fullfact.-org/articles/gender_pay_gap_how_is_britain_-fairing-28594 (last accessed on 15 July 2013).

19 See Mark Stuart and Miguel Martinez Lucio, 'Employment Relations and the UK Finance Industry: Between Globalisation and Re-regulation', Centre for Employment Relations Innovation and Change Working Paper 1 (September 2008). Available at: http://lub-swww.leeds.ac.uk/fileadmin/user_upload/Pub-lications/CERIC__WP1_Stuart_Lucio-PDF.pdf (last accessed on 2 July 2013).

20 See Equality and Human Rights Commission, 'How Fair Is Britain?', EHRC Triennial Review 1 (2010). Available at: http://www.equality-humanrights.com/keyprojects/how-fair-is-britain (last accessed on 2 July 2013).

21 The smallest gender pay gap in these islands is in Northern Ireland where the biggest source of employment is the highly unionized public sector.

22 The implementation followed a recommendation by the Prices and Income Board.

23 M. W. Gilman, 'New Single Status Deal for Council Workers', European Industrial Relations Observatory. Available at: http://www.-eurofound.europa.eu/eiro/1997/03/inbrief/-uk9703119n.htm (last accessed on 15 July 2013).

24 See London Equal Value Steering Group (Level), *A Question of Earnings: A Study of the Earnings of Blue Collar Employees in London Local Authorities* (London: LEVEL, 1987).

25 Jennifer Eady and Kara Loraine, 'Local Government Equal Pay: An Overview of Recent Case Law', *Equal Opportunities Review* 198 (2010): 11–13.

26 See UK Supreme Court Judgement, Birming-
    ham City Council vs Abdulla and Others.
    Available at: http://www.supremecourt.gov.uk/-
    decidedcases/docs/UKSC_2012_0008_Judg-
    ment.pdf (last accessed on 7 August 2013).

27 Sophie Gamwell, 'Council Workers Win
    Equal Pay Appeal', European Industrial Rela-
    tions Observatory Online (12 March 2013).
    Available at: http://www.eurofound.europa.-
    eu/eiro/2012/11/articles/uk1211019i.htm (last
    accessed on 7 August 2013).

28 Neil Elkes, 'Birmingham Council "Gagging
    Staff"over Equal Pay', *Birmingham Mail* (7
    July 2013).

29 'Solicitor Furious over Parasite Claim', *Sunder-
    land Echo* (7 Feb 2007). Available at http://-
    www.sunderlandecho.com/news/local/all-news/
    solicitor-furious-over-parasite-claim-11130168
    (last accessed on 7 August 2013).

30 Eliane Vogel-Polsky, telephone interview
    with author, 8 February 2011.

31 For comprehensive statistics and analysis, see
    Trades Union Congress, 'Closing the Gender
    Pay Gap' (London: TUC, 2008). Available at:

http://%www.tuc.org.uk/equality/tuc-14435-f0.pdf (last accessed on 7 August 2013); and Damian Grimshaw and Jill Rubery, 'Undervaluing Women's Work', Working Paper Series No 53 (UK: EOC 2007).

32 Pat Thane, 'The Scandal of Women's Pensions in Britain: How Did it Come About?' (March 2006). Available at: http://www.historyandpolicy.org/papers/policy-paper-42.html (last accessed on 2 July 2013).

33 Grimshaw and Rubery, 'Undervaluing Women's Work', p. 74.

34 European Commission, *Report on Equality between Women and Men* 2008 (Brussels: European Union, 2008), p. 8.

35 Francine Blau and Lawrence Kahn, 'The US Gender Pay Gap in the 1990s: Slowing Convergence', *Industrial and Labor Relations Review* 60(1) (2006): 43–66; here, p. 1.

36 International Labour Organization, *Women in Labour Markets: Measuring Progress and Identifying Challenges* (Geneva: International Labour Office, 2010), p. xiv.

37 Ibid., pp. xii–xiv.

38 For histories of this great struggle, see Barbara Taylor, *Eve and the New Jerusalem: Socialism and Feminism in the 19th Century* (London: Virago, 1983); Leonore Davidoff and Catherine Hall, *Family Fortunes: Men and Women of the English Middle Class, 1780–1850* (London: Hutchinson, 1987).

39 In the late 1970s and early 80s, the women's liberation journal *Red Rag* proposed a feminist economic agenda that had at its heart a single parent working part-time: Sort it for her, we believed, and you sort it for everyone.

40 See James Plunkett, 'The Missing Million: The Potential for Female Employment to Raise Living Standards in Low to Middle Income Britain' (12 December 2011). Available at: http://www.resolutionfoundation.org/media/media/downloads/The_Missing_Million.pdf (last accessed on 2 July 2013).

41 It took a heroic woman union member, Rachel Sharma, acting without union support, to challenge employers' historic tendency to cut part-timers' hours to cut costs: see Employment Appeal Tribunal judgement, Appeal No UKEAT/0561/07/RN.

42 This is the question asked by Oriel Sullivan in *Changing Gender Relations, Changing Families: Tracing the Pace of Change Over Time* (Lanham, MD: Rowman and Littlefield, 2006).

43 See Man Yee Kan and Jonathan Gershuny, 'Gender and Time Use over the Life Course' in M. Brynin and E. John (eds), *Changing Relationships* (London: Routledge, 2008), pp. 146–60; Sullivan, *Changing Gender Relations*.

44 Kan and Gershuny, 'Gender and Time Use over the Life Course', p. 147.

45 Figures taken from Jonathan Gershuny and Man Yee Kan, 'Halfway to Gender Equality in Paid and Unpaid Work? Evidence from the Multinational Time-Use Study' in Jacqueline Scott, Shirley Dex and Anke C. Plagnol (eds), *Gendered Lives: Gender Inequalities in Production and Reproduction* (Gloucestershire: Edward Elgar Publishing, 2012), pp. 74–94; Man Yee Kan, Oriel Sullivan and Jonathan Gershuny, 'Gender Convergence and Domestic Work: Discerning the Effects of Interactional and Institutional Barriers in Large-Scale Data', *Sociology* 45(2): 234–51.

See also, Anna Coote, Andrew Simms, Jane Franklin, '21 Hours' (13 February 2013), New Economics Foundation website. Available at: http://www.neweconomics.org/pages-/what-we-do (last accessed on 7 August 2013).

46 See the minutes of evidence of the examination of witnesses by the Treasury Committee on the issue of banking crisis in the UK. Available at: http://www.publications.parliament.-uk/pa/cm200809/cmselect/cmtreasy/144/0902-2606.htm (last accessed on 2 July 2013).

47 See City of London Corporation, *Childcare Sufficiency Assessment 2011* (London: City of London Corporation, 2011).

48 See Noriko O. Tsuya, Larry L Bumpass, Minja Kim Choe, 'Gender Employment and Housework in Japan, South Korea and the US', *Review of Population and Social Policy* 9 (2000): 195–220.

49 See United Nations Department of Economic and Social Affairs, *World Population Prospects*: *The 2006 Revision*; *Comprehensive Tables* (Geneva: United Nations Publications, 2007).

50 Patricia Hewitt, *About Time*: *The Revolution in Work and Family Life* (London: Rivers Oram Press, 1993).

51 Xiao-Yuan Dong and Xinli An, 'Gender Patterns and the Value of Unpaid Work: Findings from China's First Large-Scale Time Use Survey', United Nations Research Institute for Social Development Research Paper 6 (Geneva: UNRISD, 2012), p. 15. Available at: http://www.unrisd.org/publications/dong-and-an (last accessed on 7 August 2013).

52 See Anneli Anttonen, 'The Welfare State and Social Citizenship' in Kaisa Kauppinen-Toropainen and Tuula Gordon (eds), *Unresolved Dilemmas*: *Women, Work and the Family in the United States, Europe and the Former Soviet Union* (Aldershot: Ashgate, 1997), pp. 9–32.

53 See Katja Repo, 'Families, Work and Home Care: Assessing the Finnish Child Home Care Allowance', *Barn* 1 (2010): 43–61; Anne Lise Ellingsaeter and Arnlaug Leira (eds), *Politicising Parenthood in Scandinavia*: *Gender Relations in Welfare States* (Bristol, UK: Policy Press, 2006); Minna Salmi and Johanna

Lammi-Taskula, *Current Leave Policy Issues in Finland* (Helsinki: National Institute for Health and Welfare, 2009).

54 See Anna-Maija Lehto and Hanna Sutela (eds), *Threats and Opportunities*: *Findings of Finnish Quality of Work Life Surveys 1977–2003* (Helsinki: Statistics Finland, 2005).

55 See Anne Lise Ellingsaeter, *Cash for Childcare*: *Experiences from Finland, Norway and Sweden* (Bonn: Freidrich-Ebert-Stiftung, 2012).

56 Drawing on European Union protocols published in the early 1990s—'dessicated' and designed to gather dust, until they were animated by feminist activists in Northern Ireland, where they became part of The Good Friday Agreement, the treaty that ended the armed conflict in 1998. See Beatrix Campbell, *Agreement*: *The State, Conflict and Change in Northern Ireland* (London: Lawrence and Wishart, 2007).

57 See Doreen Massey, *World City* (Cambridge, UK: Polity Press, 2007).

58 See Doreen Massey, *Space, Place and Gender* (Cambridge, UK: Polity Press, 1994).

59 See Larissa Hjorth, 'Playing at Being Mobile: Gaming and Cute Culture in South Korea', *Fibreculture Journal* 8 (August 2006). Available at: http://eight.fibreculturejournal.org/fcj-052-playing-at-being-mobile-gaming-and-cute-culture-in-south-korea/ (last accessed on 2 July 2013); Florence Chee, 'Understanding Korean Experiences of Online Game Hype, Identity and the Menace of the Wang-tta', *International Journal of Media and Culture* 4(3) (2006): 225–39.

60 See Guy Standing, *Precariat: The New Dangerous Class* (London: Bloomsbury, 2011).

61 Anita Gardner, 'Landmark victory for precarious workers at Kiryung Electronics in Korea' (5 November 2010), International Metalworker's Federation website. Available at: http://www.imfmeta.org/index.cfm?c=246-02&l=2 (last accessed on 2 July 2013).

62 Kim Kwang-soo, 'Kim Jin-suk Returns after a 309-Day Miracle on the Precipice', *Hankyoreh* (11 November 2011). Available at: http://www.hani.co.kr/arti/english_edition/e_national/505030.html (last accessed on 18 July 2013).

63 'South Korea: Two Rights Defenders Facing Legal Suppression' (29 March 2012), Asian Human Rights Commission website. Available at: http://www.humanrights.asia/news/-urgent-appeals/AHRC-UAC-055-2012 (last accessed on 7 August 2013).

64 Tammy Ko Robinson, 'South Korea's 300 Day Aerial Sit-in Strike Highlights Plight of Precarious Workers in Korea and the Philippines', *Asia-Pacific Journal: Japan Focus* 9(45) (7 November 2011). Available at: http://www.-japanfocus.org/tammy_ko-Robinson/3644 (last accessed on 7 August 2013).

65 Sook-yeon Won, 'Gendered Working Time Arrangements and the Political Implications: Korean Experiences', *Time and Society* 21 (25 July 2012): 285–307.

66 See Hjorth, 'Playing at Being Mobile'.

67 See Hyeryoug Ok, 'New Media Practises in Korea', *International Journal of Communications* 5 (2011): 320–48; here, p. 327.

68 Anne Allison, 'Cuteness as Japan's Millennial Product' in Joseph Tobin (ed.), *Pikachu's Global Adventure: The Rise and Fall of Pokémon*

(Durham, NC: Duke University Press, 2004), pp. 34–49; here, p. 36.

69 Hyegong Yoo, 'The Candlelight Girls' Playground: Nationalism and the Art of Dialogy, The 2008 Candlelight Protests in South Korea', *Invisible Culture* 15 (2010). Available at: http://www.rochester.edu/in_visible_culture-/Issue_15/articles/yoo/yoo.html (last accessed on 7 August 2013).

70 See Ruth Holliday and Jo Elfving-Hwang, 'Gender, Globalization and Aesthetic Surgery in South Korea', *Body and Society* 18(2) (June 2012): 58–81.

71 See Susie Orbach, *Bodies* (London: Profile Books, 2009).

72 Max Blumenthal, 'Day of the Dead' (4 December 2012), Salon.com. Available at: http://www.salon.com/2002/12/04/juarez/ (last accessed on 3 August 2013).

73 Priscilla Connolly, 'Mexico City: Our Common Future?', *Environment and Urbanization* 11(1) (April 1999): 53–78; here, p. 56.

74 Meredith Blake, 'The Exchange: Charles Bowden on Juárez, "Murder City"', *New Yorker* (24 May 2010).

75 See Enrique Desmond Arias and Daniel M. Goldstein (eds), *Violent Democracies in Latin America* (Durham, NC: Duke University Press, 2010).

76 Laurence Burgorgue-Larsen and Amaya Ubeda de Torres, 'Case of Gonzalez et al. (Cotton Field) vs Mexico, Judgement, 16 November 2009', *Inter-American Court of Human Rights*: *Case Law and Commentary* (New York: Oxford University Press, 2011), pp. 411–52.

77 Neha Dixit, 'Unlearning Submission', *Kafila* (5 January 2013). Available at: http://kafila.org/2013/01/05/unlearning-submission-neha-dixit/ (last accessed on 7 August 2013).

78 Christophe Z. Guilmoto, 'Characteristics of Sex-Ratio Imbalances in India, and Future Scenarios' (paper for the Fourth Asia Pacific Conference on Reproductive and Sexual Health and Rights, Hyderabad, India, 29–31 October 2007). Available at: http://www.unfpa.org/gender/docs/studies/india.pdf (last accessed on 2 July 2013).

79 See A. Bardia, E. Paul, S. K. Kapoor and K. Anand, 'Declining Sex Ratio: Role of Society,

Technology and Government Regulation in Faridabad District, Haryana', *National Medical Journal of India* 17(4) (July–August 2004): 207–11.

80 See Suddhasil Siddhanta, Debasish Nandy and Satish B. Agnihotri, 'Sex Ratios in India and the "Prosperity Effect"' (2007). Available at: http://iussp2005.princeton.edu/papers/-52129 (last accessed on 15 July 2013); and Christophe Z Guilmoto, 'Beyond the Billion: India's Demography at the Beginning of the Century' (Centre Population et Développement, France, November 2011). Available at: http://www.cepedorg/IMG/pdf/ceped_wp18.-pdf (last accessed on 15 July 2013).

81 Sen, 'More than 100 Million Women Are Missing', p. 66.

82 Christophe Z. Guilmoto, 'Sex-Ratio Imbalance in Asia: Trends, Consequences and Policy Responses', UNFPA report. (Paris: LPED/IRD, 2007), p. 2. Available at: http://unfpa.-org/gender/docs/studies/summaries/regional_-analysis.pdf (last accessed on 20 August 2013).

83 See Nivedita Menon, 'State/Gender/Community–Citizenship in Contemporary India',

Economic and Political Weekly 33(5) (31 January 1998): 3–10; Christophe Jaffrelot, *Dr. Ambedkar and Untouchability: Fighting the Indian Caste System* (New York: Columbia University Press, 2005).

84 The human rights organization Shakti Vahini studied cases before the courts by couples seeking protection—nearly 90 per cent of them from the young women's families; See Rohit Mullick and Neelam Raj, 'Panchayats Turn into Kangaroo Courts', *Times of India* (9 September 2007).

85 Neha Dixit, 'A Taliban of Our Very Own', *Tehelka* 6(32) (15 August 2009). Available at: http://archive.tehelka.com/story_main42.-asp?filename=Ne150809a_taliban.asp (last accessed on 2 July 2013).

86 Anchal Vohra, 'Delhi's Triple Honour Killing: Family Says "Well Done"', NDTV.com (23 June 2010). Available at: http://www.ndtv.-com/article/cities/delhi-s-triple-honour-killing-family-says-well-done-33481 (last accessed on 2 July 2013).

87 Bhanu P. Lohumi, 'Honour Killing: 6 of Girl's Kin Held Guilty', *Tribune* (25 March 2010).

88 See Avik Ghatak, 'Murder for the Sake of Honour' (19 Dec 2011). Available at: http://www.lawyersclubindia.com/articles/Murder-for-the-Sake-of-Honour4347.asp#.-UcqasD-6SBJ8 (last accessed on 2 July 2013).

89 See Tripti Nath, 'Honour Killings: Women Fight Back', *Women's Feature Service* (16 June 2010). See also, Rani Rohini Raman, 'Death Sentence in Honour-Killing Case: A Milestone', *Pragoti* (20 April 2010); Arvind Chhabra 'Honourable Justice', *India Today* (12 April 2010): 43–5; Patralekha Chatterjee, 'Honour As Strategy', *Himal Southasian* (October 2010). Available at: http://www.himalmag.com/component/content/article/377.html (last accessed on 2 July 2013); 'Honour Killing' (2011), Shakti Vahini website. Available at: http://shaktivahini.org/initiatives-/honour-killings; 'The War on Baby Girls: Gendercide', *Economist* (4 March 2010).

90 See Ravi Kant, 'Honour Killings and the Need for New Legislation' (12 July 2012),

Law Resource India website. Available at: http://indialawyers.wordpress.com/2010/07/-03/honour-killings-and-the-need-for-new-legislation/ (last accessed on 2 July 2013).

91 See Arvind Chhabra, 'A Woman Costs Rs 30,000, a Buffalo Rs 70,000', *India Today* (9 May 2011).

92 See Bina Agarwal, 'Gender and Land Rights Revisited: Exploring New Prospects via the State, Family and Market', *Journal of Agrarian Change* 3(1–2) (January–April 2003): 184–224.

93 See UN Office on Drugs and Crime (UNODC), *Global Study on Homicide: Trends, Contexts and Data* (Geneva: UNODC, 2011); Geneva Declaration Secretariat, *Global Burden of Armed Violence* (Cambridge: Cambridge University Press, 2011).

94 Sanchari Roy, 'Empowering Women: Inheritance Rights and Female Education in India' (paper delivered at the Indian Statistical Institute, New Delhi, 12 April 2011). Available at: http://www.csae.ox.ac.uk/confeences/2011-EDiA/papers/367-Roy.pdf (last accessed on 2 July 2013).

95 See Chatterjee, 'Honour as a Strategy'.

96 See P. Sanaith, 'Farm Suicides Rise in Maharashtra, State Still Leads the List', *Hindu* (3 July 2012).

97 Jayati Ghosh, 'The Challenge of Ensuring Full Employment in the Twenty-first Century', *Indian Journal of Labour Economics* 54(1) (2011): 51–68; here, p. 52.

98 See Jayati Ghosh, *Never Done and Poorly Paid*: *Women's Work in Globalising India* (New Delhi: Women Unlimited, 2009); Indrani Mazumdar and N. Neetha, 'Employment Trends in India 1993–94 to 2009–10', Occasional Paper 59 (New Delhi: Centre for Women's Development, 2011), pp. 1–27. Available at http://-www.cwds.ac.in/OCPaper/OcasionalPaper-_56.pdf (last accessed on 2 July 2013).

99 Mazumdar and Neetha, 'Employment Trends in India 1993–94 to 2009–10', p. 12.

100 See Katrin Benhold, 'The Best Countries to Be a Woman—and the Worst' (13 June 2012). Available at: http://rendezvous.blogs.nytimes.-com/2012/06/13/the-best-countries-to-be-a-woman-and-the-worst/ (last accessed on 2 July 2013).

101 Jayati Ghosh, 'Women, Labour and Capital Accumulation in Asia', World Forum for Alternatives website. Available at: http://www.-forumdesalternatives.org/en/women-labor-and-capital-accumulation-in-asia (last accessed on 2 July 2013).

102 See Ching Kwan Lee, *Gender and the South China Miracle* (Berkeley: University of California Press, 2009).

103 See Delia Davin, *Woman-Work: Women and the Party in Revolutionary China* (Oxford: Clarendon Press, 1976); Gail Hershatter, *Women in China's Long Twentieth Century* (Berkeley: University of California Press, 2007); Lisa Rofel, *Other Modernities: Gendered Yearnings in China After Socialism* (Berkeley: University of California Press, 1999); Wang Zhen, '"State Feminism"? Gender and Socialist State Formation in Maoist China', *Feminist Studies* 7(31)(3) (2005): 519–51.

104 See Hershatter, *Women in China's Long Twentieth Century*.

105 Rofel, *Other Modernities*, p. 19.

106 See Gail Hershatter, *The Gender of Memory*: *Rural Women and China's Collective Past* (Berkeley: University of California Press, 2011).

107 When 'China Rules the World', both ignore and condemn feminist insights. See Martin Jacques, *When China Rules the World*: *The End of the Western World and the Birth of a New Global Order* (New York: Allen Lane, 2009), p. 144.

108 See He Dan, 'Women Still Face Bias on the Job, Survey Finds' (22 October 2011). Available at: http://www.china-daily.com.cn/biz-china/2011-10/22/content_13954171.htm (last accessed on 2 July 2013).

109 See Dong and An, 'Gender Patterns and Values of Unpaid Work'.

110 Arvind Subramanian, 'What is China Doing to its Workers', *Business Standard* (8 Feb 2008). Debated by Dali L. Yang in 'Whither the Patterns of Development in China?' (Beijing Chicago Council on Global Affairs, 2012), pp. 42–5. Available at: http://www.thechicago-council.org/UserFiles/File/Task%20Force%-

20Reports/2012_Global_Economy/Yang-_Development_in_China.pdf (last accessed on 3 August 2013).

111 See Fenglian Du and Xiao-yuan Dong, 'Women's Labour Force Participation and Childcare Choices in Urban China During the Economic Transition' (working paper for the Department of Economics, University of Winnipeg, October 2010).

112 Sarah Cook and Xiao-yuan Dong, 'Harsh Choices and Chinese Women's Paid Work and Unpaid Care Responsibilities' in Shahra Razavi (ed.), *Seen, Heard and Counted: Rethinking Care in a Development Context* (Oxford: Wiley Blackwell, 2012), pp. 73–91; here, pp. 80, 85.

113 See Delia Davin, *Internal Migration in Contemporary China* (London: Palgrave, 1999); Harriet Evans and Julia C. Strauss (eds), *Gender in Flux: Agency and Its Limits in Contemporary China* (Cambridge: Cambridge University Press, 2011).

114 Students and Scholars against Corporate Misbehaviour (SACOM), 'Foxconn and Apple Fail to Fulfil Promises: Predicaments of Workers

After the Suicides' (6 May 2011). Available at: http://sacom.hk/archives/849 (last accessed on 2 July 2013); Charles Duhigg and David Barboza, 'In China Human Costs are Built into an iPad', *New York Times* (25 January 2012); SACOM, 'Workers as Machines: Military Management in Foxconn' (13 October 2010). Available at: http://sacom.hk/archives/740 (last accessed on 2 July 2013); Jenny Chan and Ngai Pun, 'Suicide as Protest for the New Generation of Chinese Migrant Workers: Foxconn, Global Capital, and the State', *Asia-Pacific Journal: Japan Focus* 37(2) (September 2010). Available at: http://japanfocus.org/-jenny-chan/3408 (last accessed on 7 August 2013).

115 Jean-Phillipe Beja, 'The New Working Class Renews the Repertoire of Class Conflict' (Elizabeth Guill trans.), *China Perspectives* 2 (2011): 3–7; here, pp. 4–5; Yu Jianrong, 'Maintaining a Baseline of Social Stability' (3 April 2010). Available at http://chinastudygroup.net/2010/-04/yu-jianrong-on-maintaining-a-baseline-of-social-stability/ (last accessed on 2 July 2013); see also Ching Kwan Lee and Yuan Shen, 'China: The Paradox and Possibility of Public

Labor Sociology in China', *Work and Occupations* 36(2) (May 2009): 110–25.

116 See Ching Kwan Lee, *Against the Law–Labor Protests in China's Rustbelt and Sunbelt* (University of California Press, 2007).

117 Iris Marion Young, *Throwing Like a Girl and Other Essays in Feminist Philosophy and Social Theory* (Bloomington, IN: Indiana University Press, 1990), p. 155; Sandra Lee Bartky, *Femininity and Domination*: *Studies in the Phenomenology of Oppression* (London: Routledge, 1990), p. 80. See also Iris Marion Young, *Justice and the Politics of Difference* (Princeton, NJ: Princeton University Press, 1990); Kumkum Sangari, *Politics of the Possible* (London: Anthem Press, 2002); Susan Bordo, *Unbearable Weight*: *Feminism, Western Culture and the Body* (Berkeley: University of California Press, 1993).

118 Alba Zaluar, 'Unfinished Democratisation: the Failure of Public Safety', *Estudos Avancados* 21(61) (2007): 31–49; Tatiana Moura, 'Between Micro-war and Macro-peace' (paper for 'Hegemonic Masculinities in International Politics' conference, Manchester University, 2005). Available at: http://www.-

eurozine.com/articles/2007-06-28-moura-en.html (last accessed 9 July 2013); see also Beatrix Campbell, *Goliath–Britain's Dangerous Places* (London: Methuen, 1994); James Messerschmidt, *Masculinities and Crime: Critique and Reconceptualisation of Theory* (Lanham, MD: Rowman and Littlefield, 1993).

119 See Massey, *World City*; Mike Davies, *Planet of Slums* (London: Verso, 2006); Saskia Sassen, *The Global City* (New York: Princeton University Press, 2001); Zaluar, 'Unfinished Democratisation: the Failure of Public Safety'.

120 Enrique Desmond Arias and Daniel M. Goldstein, 'Violent Pluralism: Understanding Democracies in Latin America' in Arias and Goldstein (eds), *Violent Democracies in Latin America* (Durham, NC: Duke University Press, 2010), pp. 1–34; here, p. 4; See Daniel M. Goldstein, 'Flexible Justice: Neo-Liberal Violence and "Self-Help" Security in Bolivia', *Critique of Anthropology* 25(4) (December 2005): 389–411.

121 See Evan Williams, 'Death to Undesirables: Brazil's Murder Capital', *Independent* (15 May 2009).

122 See John Kampfner, *Blair's Wars* (London: Free Press, 2003).

123 See Mary Kaldor, *New and Old War and Organised Violence in a Global Era* (Cambridge, UK: Polity Press, 1999); 1.5 billion people live in conflict zones, according to World Bank, *World Development Report: Conflict, Security and Development* (Washington DC: World Bank Publications, 2011).

124 Mary Kaldor, 'Beyond Militarism, Arms Races and Arms Control' (essay prepared for the Nobel Peace Prize Centennial Symposium, Oslo, 6–8 December 2001). Available at: http://essays.ssrc.org/sept11/essays/kaldor.htm (last accessed on 2 July 2013).

125 Adam Hochschild, *King Leopold's Ghost: A Story of Greed, Terror and Heroism in Colonial Africa* (New York: Mariner, 1999).

126 See Benjamin Coghlan, Richard J Brennan, Pascal Ngoy, David Dofara, Brad Otto, Mark Clements and Tony Stewart, 'Mortality in the Democratic Republic of Congo: A Nationwide Survey', *Lancet* 367 (January 2006): 44–51. Available at: http://conflict.lshtm.ac.uk/media/-

DRC_mort_2003_2004_Coghlan_Lancet_-2006.pdf (last accessed on 7 August 2013).

127 See Trust Law, 'Factsheet: The World's Most dangerous Countries for Women'. Available at: http://www.trust.-org/trustlaw/news/factsheet-the-worlds-most-dangerous-countries-for-women (last accessed on 2 July 2013).

128 See 'Report of the International Committee of the Red Cross on the Treatment of the Coalition Forces of Prisoners of War and Other Protected Persons by the Geneva Conventions in Iraq During Arrest, Internment and Interrogation' (February 2004). Available at: http://-www.derechos.org/nizkor-/us/doc/-icrc-prisoner-report-feb-2004.-pdf (last accessed on 2 July 2013).

129 See Peter Beaumont, 'The Hidden Victims of a Brutal Conflict: Iraq's Women', *Observer* (6 October 2006).

130 See Cynthia Enloe and Helen Benedict, *Lonely Soldiers* (London: Random House, 2010).

131 See Geneva Declaration Secretariat, *Global Burden of Armed Violence* (Cambridge: Cambridge University Press, 2011); UNODC,

Global Study on Homicide: *Trends, Contexts and Data* (Geneva: UNODC, 2011).

132 International Crisis Group, 'Violence and Politics in Venezuela', Latin America Report 38 (Bogotá/ Brussels: ICG, 2011). Available at: http://www.crisisgroup.org/~/media/Files-/latinamerica/venezuela/38%20Violence%20-and%20Politics%20in%20Venezuela.pdf (last accessed on 2 July 2013).

133 See Francisco Guttierez Sanin and Anna Maria Jaramillo, 'Crime, (Counter-)insurgency and the Privatization of Security—the Case of Medellin, Colombia', *Environment and Urbanization* 16(3) (2004): 17–30.

134 See Cynthia Enloe, *Maneuvers: The International Politics of Militarizing Women's Lives* (Berkeley, Los Angeles: University of California Press, 2000); James W. Messerschmidt, *Masculinities and Crime: Critique and Reconceptualization of Theory* (Lanham, MD: Rowman and Littlefield, 1993).

135 Wendy Brown, *States of Injury: Power and Freedom in Late Modernity* (Princeton, NJ: Princeton University Press, 1995); Naomi Wolf, *Fire*

with Fire: *The New Female Power and How to Use It* (London: Vintage Books, 1994).

136 See Judith Lewis Herman, *Trauma and Recovery* (New York: Basic Books, 1992).

137 The concept emerged in the US women's liberation movement at the end of the 1960s. See http://www.carolhanisch.org/CHwritings-/PIP.html (last accessed on 2 July 2013); See Susan Bordo, 'Feminism, Foucault and the Politics of the Body' in Caroline Ramazanoglu, *Up against Foucault*: *Explorations of Some Tensions between Foucault and Feminism* (London: Routledge, 2003), pp. 179–202.

138 Roy Greenslade, 'Forty Years On—The Soaraway Sun is Still Setting the Political Agenda' (17 November 2009). Available at: http://-www.guardian.co.uk/media/greenslade/2009/-nov/17/sun-rupert-murdoch (last accessed on 7 August 2013).

139 Evidence of Sue Akers, Assistant Chief Constable, Metropolitan Police London, to the Leveson Inquiry, 12 February 2012.

140 Sally Hamilton, 'How Rich is Britain's No. 1 Reality Star Katie Price?' *Mail Online* (8 June

2011). Available at: http://www.thisismoney.-co.uk/money/article-1724142/How-rich-Katie-Price.html (last accessed on 7 August 2013).

141 See Maddy Coy and Maria Garner, 'Glamour Modelling and the Marketing of Self-Sexualization: Critical Reflections', *International Journal of Cultural Studies* 13(6) (2010): 657–75.

142 Decca Aitkenhead, 'Katie Price: "People think I'm Not Normal"', *Guardian* (16 August 2010).

143 Robert Coleville, 'The Economic Power of Pornography', *Telegraph* (5 March 2007).

144 Coy and Garner, 'Glamour Modelling and the Marketing of Self-Sexualization', p. 663.

145 See Edward Said, *Orientalism* (New York: Vintage Books, 1979); Linda Nochlin, 'The Imaginary Orient', *Art in America* (May 1983); Rana Kabbani, *Imperial Fictions: Europe's Myth of the Orients* (Bloomington, IN: Indiana University Press, 1986).

146 See Sylvie Tissot, 'Excluding Muslim Women: From Hijab to Niqab, from School to Public Spaces', *Public Culture* 23(1) (2011): 39–46.

147 Joan Wallach Scott, *The Politics of the Veil* (Princeton, NJ: Princeton University Press, 2011), p. 55.

148 Ibid.

149 Haleh Ashfar, 'Can I see Your Hair? Choice, Agency and Attitudes: The Dilemma of Faith and Feminism for Muslim Women Who Cover', *Ethnic and Racial Studies* 31(2) (February 2008): 411–27.

150 Rahila Gupta, 'We Don't Need Hegel: The Burka is a Cloth Soaked in Blood', *Guardian* (8 July 2009).

151 John Berger, *Ways of Seeing* (London: Penguin, 1972), p. 54

152 Rosemary Betterton, 'Why Is My Art Not as Good as Me?: Femininity, Feminism, and Life-Drawing in Tracey Emin's Art' in Mandy Merck and Chris Townsend (eds), *The Art of Tracey Emin* (London: Thames and Hudson, 2002), pp. 22–39; here, p. 27.

153 Tracey Emin, 'This is Another Place', exhibition catalogue (Oxford: Modern Art, 2003).

154 See Tim Walker, 'Charles Saatchi Is in Love with Nigella Lawson, Says Tracey Emin', *Telegraph* (20 June 2013).

155 Quoted in Thomas Kiernan, *Repulsion: The Life and Times of Roman Polanski* (London: New English Library, 1981), p. 260.

156 See Martin Amis, 'Interview: Roman Polanski', *Observer* (6 December 2009).

157 At the same time, Italian prime minister Silvio Berlusconi was under investigation for complicity in prostitution.

158 Francoise-Marie Santucci, 'Les 1001 Vies de Zahia (The 1001 Lives of Zahia)', *Libération Next* (7 February 2010) (my translation). Avaialable at: http://next.liberation.fr/mode-/-01012388449-les-1001-vies-de-zahia (last accessed on 2 July 2013).

159 Ibid.

160 Ibid.

161 See Chris Atmore, 'Victims, Backlash, and Radical Feminist Theory (Or the Morning after They Stole Feminism's Fire)' in Sharon Lamb (ed.), *New Versions of Victims: Feminists Struggle with the Concept* (London and New York: New York University Press, 1999), pp. 183–212.

162 See Gilbert Wondracek, Thorsten Holz, Christian Platzer, Engin Kirda and Christopher Kruegel, 'Is the Internet for Porn? An Insight into the Online Industry' (paper presented at

the Ninth Workshop on the Economics of Information Security, Harvard University, Cambridge, MA, 7–8 June 2010). Available at: http://iseclab.org/papers/-weis2010.pdf (last accessed on 2 July 2013).

163 See Catherine Hakim, *Honey Money*: *The Power of Erotic Capital* (London: Allen Lane, 2011); Laurie Penny, *Meat Market*: *Female Flesh under Capitalism* (London: Zero Books, 2011).

164 Blog by the director of Pathways of Women's Empowerment, Andrea Cornwall, *Guardian* (26 July 2012).

165 Quoted in Christine Overall, 'What's Wrong with Prostitution? Evaluating Sex Work', *Signs* 17(4) (1992): 705–24; here, p. 706.

166 See Hakim, *Honey Money*.

167 Stuart Hall, 'Gramsci's Relevance for the Study of Race and Ethnicity', *Journal of Communication Enquiry* 10(5) (1986): 5–27.

168 Penny, *Meat Market*, p. 18.

169 Laurie Penny quoted in Global Comment, 'Feminism, Socialism and the Meat Market: An Interview With Laurie Penny'. Available at http://globalcomment.com/feminism-social-

ism-and-the-meat-market-an-interview-with-laurie-penny/ (last accessed on 2 July 2013).

170 See Maddy Coy, Miranda Horvath, Liz Kelly, 'It's Just Like Going to the Supermarket: Men Buying Sex in East London', Report by Child and Woman Abuse Studies Unit (CWASU) (London Metropolitan University, 2007); Melissa Fairly, Julie Bindel, Jaqueline M. Golding, *Men Who Buy Sex*: *Who They Buy and What They Know* (London: Eaves, 2009); Jane Pitcher, Maggie O'Neill, Teela Sanders, *Prostitution, Sex Work, Policy Politics* (London: Sage, 2009).

171 Sone Hiromi, 'Prostitution and Public Authority' (Terashima Akiko and Anne Walthall trans) in Hitomi Tonomura, Anne Walthall, Wakita Haruko (eds), *Women and Class in Japanese History* (Anne Arbor: Centre of Japanese Studies, University of Michigan, 1999), pp. 169–85; Miriam Silverberg, *Erotic, Grotesque Nonsense*: *The Mass Culture of Japanese Modern Times* (Berkeley and Los Angeles: University of California Press, 2009); Elizabeth S. Cohen, 'Seen and Known: Prostitutes in the Cityscape of Late Sixteenth-Century

Rome', *Renaissance Studies* 12(3) (1998): 392–409; Gail Hershatter, *Dangerous Pleasures: Prostitution and Modernity in Twentieth Century Shanghai* (Berkeley and Los Angeles: University of California Press, 1999); Cynthia Enloe, *Maneuvers: The International Politics of Militarizing Women's Lives* (Berkeley and Los Angeles: University of California Press, 2000); Rohini Sahni and V. Kalyan Shankar, *The First Pan-India Survey of Sex Workers* (Mumbai: Center for Advocacy on Stigma and Marginalisation, 2011). Available at: http://www.sangram.org/resources/Pan_India_Survey_of_-Sex_workers.pdf (last accessed on 2 July 2013).

172 See Carole Pateman, 'Defending Prostitution: Charges Against Ericsson', *Ethics* 93(3) (April 1983): 561–5. See what men themselves say in Coy, Horvath, Kelly, 'It's Just Like Going to the Supermarket'; Fairley, Bindel, Golding, *Men Who Buy Sex*.

173 Pateman, 'Defending Prostitution', p. 562.

174 ILO, *ILO Action against Trafficking in Human Beings* (Geneva: ILO, 2008).

175 Ibid., p. 11.

176 See ILO, *Harder to See Harder to Count: Survey Guidelines to Estimate Forced Labour of Adults and Children* (Geneva: ILO, 2012).

177 ILO, *ILO Action against Trafficking in Human Beings*, p. 17.

178 Dori Laub and Shoshana Felman, *Testimony: Crises of Witnessing in Literature, Psychoanalysis, and History* (London: Routledge, 1992).

179 See Liz Kelly, Jo Lovett, Linda Regan, 'A Gap or a Chasm? Attrition Rates in Reported Rape Cases', Home Office Research Study 293 (2005).

180 See Betsy Stanko, Jenny Norman and Daniela Wunsch, 'The Attrition of Rape Allegations in London: A Review' (London: Metropolitan Police Survey, 2007).

181 This pattern was cruelly exposed in two scandals in 2012: the exploitation of around 50 girls by a ring of men in Greater Manchester, denigrated as prostitutes by police and social services; 'national treasure' TV celebrity Jimmy Savile's predatory trail that targeted prisoners, patients, children in care and his fans.

182 See Beatrix Campbell, 'The Truth About Rape', *New Statesman* (7 April 2007).

183 See Evidence of Brian Paddick to Leveson Inquiry, 27 February 2012. Available at: http://www.levesoninquiry.org.uk/wp-content/uploads/2012/02/lev-270212am.pdf (last accessed on 2 July 2013).

184 Cheryl Thomas, 'Are Juries Fair?', Ministry of Justice Research Series 1 (2010).

185 See HMIC and HMCPSI, 'Forging the Links: Rape Investigation and Prosecution' (2012). Available at: http://www.hmic.gov.uk/media/-forging-the-links-rape-investigation-and-prosecution-20120228.pdf (last accessed on 2 July 2013); Miranda Horvath, Stephen Tong, Emma Williams, 'An Overview of Reform in England and Wales', *Journal of Criminal Justice Research* 1(2) (2011): 1–18; Jennifer Brown, Miranda Horvath, Liz Kelly, Nicole Westmoreland, *Connections and Disconnections: Assessing Evidence, Knowledge and Practice in Response to Rape* (London: Government Equalities Office, 2010).

186 Evidence to US Senate Judiciary Committee hearings: The Chronic Failure to Report and

Investigate Rape Cases (14 September 2010). Available at: http://www.judiciary.senate.gov/-pdf/09-14-10%20Tracy%20Testimony.pdf (last accessed on 2 July 2013); Jo Lovett and Liz Kelly, 'Different Systems, Similar Outcomes: Tracking Attrition in Reported Rape Cases Across Europe', Final Research Report by CWASU and European Commission, 2009. See also evidence to the US Senate Judiciary Committee.

187 See Lovett and Kelly, 'Different Systems, Similar Outcomes: Tracking Attrition in Reported Rape Cases Across Europe', p. 112.

188 See Dixit, 'Unlearning Submission'.

189 See HMIC and HMCPSI, *Forging the Links*.

190 See Carole Pateman, 'Women and Consent' in *The Disorder of Women: Democracy, Feminism, and Political Theory* (Cambridge, UK: Polity Press, 1989), pp. 71–89.

191 Judith Lewis Herman, 'Justice from the Victims' Perspective', *Violence Against Women* 11(5) (2005): 571–602; here, p. 571.

192 See Mahmood Mamdani, 'Reconciliation without Justice'. Available at: http://web.uct.-

ac.za/depts/sarb/X0045_Mamdani.html; Julie Mertus, 'Truth in a Box: The Limits of Justice Through Judicial Mechanisms' in Ifi Amadiume and Abdullahi An-Na'im (eds), *The Politics of Memory: Truth, Healing and Social Justice* (London: Zed Books, 2000), pp. 142–61.

193 Christine Bell and Catherine O'Rourke, 'Peace Agreements or Pieces of Paper: UN Security Council Resolution 1325 and Peace Negotiations and Agreements', Research Paper 1 (Transitional Justice Institute, University of Ulster, 2011).

194 Judith Lewis Herman, 'Justice from the Victims' Perspective', p. 599.

195 See Veena Das, 'Listening to Voices', *Alterites* 7(1) (2010): 136–45.

196 See Veena Das and Arthur Kleinman, 'Introduction' in Veena Das, Arthur Kleinman, Margaret Lock, Mamphela Ramphele and Pamela Reynolds (eds), *Remaking a World: Violence, Social Suffering and Recovery* (Berkeley and Los Angeles: University of California Press, 2001), pp. 1–30; here, p. 20.

197 See Alyson Manda Cole, *The Cult of True Victimhood: From the War on Welfare to the War on Terror* (Stanford: Stanford University Press, 2007); Alison Convery, 'No Victims, No Oppression: Feminist Theory and the Denial of Victimhood' (paper delivered at Australasian Political Studies Association, University of Newcastle, 25 to 27 September 2006).

198 Herman, 'Justice from the Victims' Perspective', p. 599.